How to Do Your Best on Every Test

Test-Taking Skills for Elementary Students

Jolie S. Brams, Ph.D.

Show What You Know® Publishing
A Division of Englefield & Associates, Inc.
Columbus, OH U.S.A.

Published by:
Show What You Know® Publishing
A Division of Englefield & Associates, Inc.
P.O. Box 341348
Columbus, OH 43234-1348
Phone: 614-764-1211
www.showwhatyouknowpublishing.com

Printed in the United States of America
05 04 03   20 19 18 17 16 15 14 13 12 11 10 9 8 7 6 5 4 3 2 1

ISBN: 1-59230-027-8

About the Author

For 25 years, Dr. Jolie S. Brams, a clinical psychologist, has been helping children and families lead happier lives.

Dr. Brams received her Bachelor's Degree in Psychology with Honors from the University of Texas and her Doctorate in Clinical Psychology, with specialization in Child Development, from Michigan State University. She was a faculty member at three medical schools, teaching medical students and residents, and a pediatric psychologist at a major children's hospital. Presently, she is an adjunct faculty member in the Department of Psychiatry at The Ohio State University.

In addition to her private psychology practice, Dr. Brams is the director of a forensic psychology consulting firm and evaluates children and adolescents for attorneys and the court system. She is a dynamic speaker who has shared her experience and enthusiasm through more than 100 presentations to parent groups, schools, and agencies. She has also been an invited guest on many local and national radio and television programs.

Dr. Brams is a contributor to the Show What You Know® line of test-preparation books. She has written chapters on test-taking strategies and reducing test anxiety for grades three through eleven. Her material appears in Show What You Know® on the Ohio Proficiency Tests, Show What You Know® on the Washington Assessment of Student Learning (WASL), Show What You Know® on the Florida Comprehensive Assessment Test (FCAT), and Show What You Know® on the Texas Assessment of Knowledge and Skills (TAKS).

Acknowledgements

Show What You Know® Publishing acknowledges the following for their efforts in making this assessment material available for students, parents, and teachers.

Cindi Englefield, President/Publisher
Eloise Boehm-Sasala, Vice President/Managing Editor
Mercedes Baltzell, Production Editor
Lainie Burke, Editor/Graphic Design, Cover Designer
Erin McDonald, Project Editor
Jennifer Harney, Illustrator
Erica T. Klingerman, Proofreader

Table of Contents

A Note for Teachers and Parents

This book is about more than taking tests. Learning these test-taking skills can help students prepare for and tackle many other challenges that they will encounter both in school and outside of the classroom. Thinking positively, using reasoning skills, valuing the importance of practice, and taking time to do a task well are all skills that can lead to confidence and success. When you review these skills with your children or students, help them understand how these skills are helpful beyond just doing better on tests.

About five years ago, I began to see an increase in the number of my young patients who were stressed by tests. Much of their stress was related to standardized testing, such as statewide proficiency testing. As the children (and teens) told their stories, it appeared that many, many young students had little idea how to approach taking tests. At the same time, I began to evaluate an increasing number of college students with test anxiety that caused them undue hardship and failure—unnecessary obstacles if they had been taught some simple test-taking strategies when they were younger. In college, their levels of anxiety were sky high, and it compounded their fears of poor performance.

Doing well in school can create a foundation for life-long positive self-esteem. Children who feel that they can do their best make better choices in other areas of their lives. Their "I can do it!" attitude helps protect them from the hopeless and angry feelings so common among children and teens who are alienated from school and society. Success in the early grades leads to success in later years.

This book is organized into nine chapters; all of them are short and entertaining. While some children may need more help then others in mastering the concepts in each chapter, the book was written so that most students from grades three to five can read the material with a reasonable degree of ease and can quickly learn the main point of each chapter. The point is that success can only lead to more success!

For a number of reasons, this book was a pleasure to write. Perhaps one of the greatest motivators for me has been my experience with the histories of children who fail. In addition to my more than 20 years directing a psychology practice and seeing thousands of patients, I evaluate juveniles who are unfortunately involved in the court system. Probably 95% of these youths began to stumble in the middle years of elementary school. They tell the same sad and very real story, "I really was a smart kid but then . . ." Now, they fear most challenges and use brawn instead of brains to get what they need.

Children have a remarkable capacity for growth. Not only do they model what they see and practice what they are taught, but they create their own ways of problem solving that should make adults envious. All they need is our support and some age-appropriate assistance to be the best that they can be. Test-taking skills are some of many "tools for life" that equip them with what it takes to be confident and competent.

So, let's give our kids every chance to "SHOW WHAT THEY KNOW!"

Who Wrote This Book?

Hi! My name is Dr. Jolie Brams, but most kids call me "Dr. Jolie." One kid calls me "DJB" (initials for Dr. Jolie Brams) and makes me laugh. It sounds kind of cool, don't you think? But I call all kids "WONDERFUL" because that is what they are!

I am not a doctor who looks in your nose or between your toes. (In fact, don't even THINK of showing me any noses, toes, or whatever!) What I do is help kids BE THE BEST THEY CAN BE! A lot of people think it is easy being a kid, but are they wrong! Kids have a hundred things to do at once . . . tell any grownup to try that! First, they have to learn . . . and learn A LOT! Did you know that you learn more in elementary school than at any other time in your life? In a few short years, you have to learn to read, write, spell, know about science, history, geography . . . WHEW, I'm tired already! Kids also have to figure out how to believe in themselves and feel good about what they do. And they have to do all of that with noisy brothers and sisters, bossy parents, and who knows what else. I think all kids should get an award every day.

My job is to help kids have happy lives. Sometimes I talk to them by themselves, and sometimes with their families, so everyone can figure out answers together. Kids and families learn and change when they work to make things better. And as for me, well, I've learned many things by helping others. One of the most important things I've learned is that kids' brains work like magic! Most of the time, if kids hear some good advice, all of a sudden their brains grow! It is really amazing. Grownups are different. I think that their brains are more stubborn. But kids say, "Hey, that's a good idea! Let's use it to solve all these problems!"

In the last few years, many kids have told me that they are worried about tests. In some states, there are tests once a year in certain grades to see how students are learning. This is hard for some kids to think about. They say to themselves, "I've had a spelling or math test before, but never a huge test like that!" They start doubting themselves. Other kids don't even like the little tests. They also worry and aren't sure if they can do well. But I know that all kids can do better on tests than they ever imagined! So I put my own brain to the test and wrote this book to help.

Every Kid Can be a Test-Taking Hero

Well, here you are. Your teacher or a parent has given you this book about taking tests. "Oh no," you might think to yourself. "Here's more stuff for me to learn. My brain can only do so much before it explodes! And it doesn't matter anyway. I could read all the books in the world and I still wouldn't be a good test taker."

STOP RIGHT THERE! You might be a great soccer-playing kid or you may be able to draw the best doodles or bake the most delicious cookies, but you are wrong about tests. You CAN do great on tests. And you won't have to have an exploding brain to do it!

You might not think about it, but you have taken tests ever since you were a little baby. "Yeah, right," you might say. "Did my grandmother test me on "goo-goo" and "baa-baa?" Well, probably not, but you tested yourself! Think about yourself as a baby, playing on the rug in your living room. You see your favorite bottle (the one with the little bears on it) up on the counter. Somehow you have to get that bottle! So you try different ways to get your grandmother's attention and let her know what you want. First you throw a toy, but all that does is get the toy taken away! Then you cry, but all she does is check your diaper! Finally, you try speaking. You use your brain to remember what "that thing with the milk in it" is called. "What did I hear Mom call it?" you ask yourself. Then you try to figure out how to say it. After saying, "buh-bub" and "tuh-tuh," you say "baa-baa." That is the right answer, at least for a baby! Not only do you get your bottle, but you also feel great about yourself! This was a test of your abilities. You had a problem to solve and you figured it out. It was an important problem too, because you were thirsty. You had to do well. That's just like a test in school. You were facing a challenge—a problem that you had to solve—and you figured out how. You might have been a little worried ("Hey, suppose I don't get that bottle?") or a little frustrated ("Why doesn't anyone listen to a baby?"), but in the end you were a success.

Throughout your life, you have been challenged to do and learn many, many things, and you have been a success at most of them! A test is just another kind of challenge. The only difference between a test and other challenges is that everyone makes a big deal over tests. (Don't ask me why, but they do!) And when everyone makes tests huge challenges, a lot of kids see tests as a monster waiting to get them. This is not good, because the bigger the monster, the more kids worry, and the harder it is to show what you know on tests!

This book will help you beat the test monster and be a test-taking hero. And it's not as hard as you think. If you want to show what you know on tests, all you have to do is know when you are worried and figure out some ways to beat that feeling. And all kids can also learn to do their best on tests by learning some simple ways to be wise test takers. You will be amazed at how well you can do! (And the test monster will soon be gone forever!)

So let's get started. This book has many chapters, but they are short . . . on purpose! It's easier to learn how to be a test hero a little bit at a time (or your brain could explode!). Each chapter gives you one tool to send that test monster on his way. In each chapter there is an exercise to help you remember what you read. (And there are some exercises just for fun!) Many chapters have stories about kids just like you and how they became test-taking heroes. You might want to start at the beginning of the book. You might want a teacher or parent to help you with each chapter as you read it, or you might want to read the chapter and do the exercise and then show what you learned to a grownup. Some kids work on a chapter every night or so, and some work through a chapter once a week. You have to figure out how you learn best. It is a good idea to learn to show what you know when you aren't sleepy or too busy! This is important stuff, and your brain needs to be ready and awake to battle that test monster!

To help you get ready to meet the test-taking challenge, think about all the challenges you have had in your life . . . and have beaten! Here is a chart to help you get started. Look at all you have done. Now it's time to win the test-taking challenge.

Nondi wrote down two times when she was a hero. Now make your own chart like she did.

I learned to ride a 2-wheel bike!		
I learned to tie my shoe!		

Chapter 1

What Kind of Test Taker Am I?

In this chapter, you are going to learn about how some people feel about tests. You may find that you feel the same way. If you do, that is OK. Use what you learn from each of these kids to help you think about tests differently. You will be surprised at how much better you will feel!

In This Chapter . . .

Activity 1

Do You Worry About Tests? You're Not Alone!

What would you rather do?

a. Play outside.
b. Listen to music.
c. Go get some ice cream.
d. Take a test.

Most likely, if you asked 1,000,000 kids this question, 999,999 would pick "a" or "b" or "c." Even kids who like tests would rather do something fun than take a test.

The good news is that taking a test does not have to be terrible! There are many things you can do to feel better about taking tests. In the chapters that follow, you will learn about how some kids worry about tests. You will see how they can find ways to worry less. Even if you don't get very stressed about tests, here is some knowledge to help you fight off the "test monster" if he ever comes your way!

It's OK to worry a little! A test is a challenge. A challenge means that we try to do something that might be hard, but not impossible. It is fine to feel like a football player waiting for the "big game." A little bit of worry helps us do better. If that football player said, "I don't care if we win or lose!" do you think he will play his best? NO! You have to care a little to show what you know.

Even though it's OK to worry a little, it's not good to worry too much. Do you think about big tests all the time? Do you feel really scared or sick before you take a test? If you do, go get help from a grownup right now! And make sure you read this book.

Here is a limerick that might help!

> There was a student named Claire,
> Who usually said, "I don't care!"
> Her sister named Bess
> Always felt total stress.
> They weren't a successful pair!

No one is perfect! Even famous people don't do their best all of the time. And some heroes have failed at things they tried. Did you know that Abraham Lincoln tried seven times to win an election? He kept losing and losing but never gave up. And look what happened! He became President and changed the history of our country!

You will feel less stress about tests when you remember that if you do not do well, you can always do better next time. Who knows, you might be the President someday!

If you know when you are stressed, you can get help! Sometimes we don't take the time to think about ourselves. We just go on and on and never take the time to see how we are feeling. One time, Erin didn't pay attention to how she felt. She was feeling hot and her head hurt a little, but she kept on playing kickball. The next day she was really sick with the flu. She was sick for 10 days. The doctor told her that if she had stopped playing and rested, she might have been well sooner.

Look at the list below. Do you have any of these thoughts or feelings? If you do, talk to a grownup!

My Thoughts and Feelings

☐ I think about tests all the time.

☐ I feel bad if I have fun because I should be studying.

☐ My stomach or head hurts when I think about tests.

☐ I can't stop thinking about how other kids do on tests.

☐ On test days, I wish I could stay home from school.

☐ If I miss one or two questions on a test, I feel badly about myself.

☐ Tests are made hard to ruin my life . . . it's not fair!

☐ If I don't do well on a test, terrible things will happen.

☐ My teacher will not like me if my test score is poor.

Activity 2

Are You Like "Worried Wendy"?

Wendy always thought that the worst would happen when she took a test. "What if the questions are too hard? What if I don't do well? I bet my teacher won't like me anymore. And my dad will be so upset, his head will pop off! He will make me study until I'm 100 years old!"

Wendy worried so much that her stomach began to hurt her every day. Her dad tried to tell her that everything would be OK, but it was hard for Wendy to stop her worried thoughts.

One night her dad came into her room with a little clock. "What in the world is he doing with that little clock?" thought Wendy. Her dad put it on her bed.

"Wendy, is that a good clock or a bad clock?" asked her dad. "I don't know" replied Wendy. Her dad then said, "Well, I think it is a bad clock. There isn't anything good about it. The numbers are small and are hard to read. It isn't pretty or fancy. And it could get lost, too."

Wendy didn't agree with her dad. "Dad, that's not a bad clock! It is kind of cute and most people can read the numbers on it just fine. Also, if you lost it, it doesn't cost much money to buy a new one. Why did you say such bad things about that clock? It looks OK to me!"

Wendy's dad gave her a hug. "Now you know that everything is in how you look at it. That clock isn't all good or all bad. It is just a clock! And, Wendy, tests aren't good or bad. Tests give you a chance to show what you know. Terrible things won't happen if you don't do well on a test." Wendy listened and felt better! Now she thinks good things about tests, not bad things. Here is what Wendy wrote!

Good Things About Tests

- Tests give me a chance to study and to learn.
- When I take a test, I can practice my test-taking skills.
- I can try to do better on each test.
- My dad might give me a reward for studying.
- I will probably do better than I ever expected!
- When I get a test back, I learn from my mistakes.

Try to Think Good Thoughts

Just as Wendy's dad showed her the little clock, find something in your room or your house and look at it. Maybe you could choose a can of soda pop, a television, or even the family car! Write down everything good and everything bad that you can think of on the chart at the bottom of the page. An example of how to fill out the chart is shown below. A fourth grader name Rachel picked popcorn. This is what she wrote.

RACHEL'S THOUGHTS ABOUT POPCORN	
Bad Things	**Good Things**
Sometimes all the corn doesn't pop.	It is easy to make.
I get messy hands when I eat it.	It tastes great!
It is very hot after it cooks.	Hot popcorn is the best!
Candy is more fun to eat.	Popcorn (without butter) is better for you.
We only get it when we watch movies.	It makes movies more fun!

MY THOUGHTS ABOUT _____	
Bad Things	**Good Things**

Activity 3

Give Yourself a Break! Don't Be Like "Perfect Pat"!

Pat thought she should spend all of her time studying. She told herself, "I should study more. I shouldn't have fun. Having fun is a waste of time."

Pat would play with her friends, but she never had a very good time. In the middle of volleyball or crafts, Pat would think, "I should be studying for my test. Or maybe I should be at home writing my book report. If I don't study all the time, I will fail for sure!"

Ms. Hernandez was the principal at Pat's school. She saw that Pat was worried all of the time. Once, Pat wanted to stay inside during recess to study. This really worried Ms. Hernandez. She knew that kids needed to have fun. So Ms. Hernandez had a talk with Pat.

"Pat," she said, "you have to stop worrying about studying and have some fun."

"But I can't," said Pat. "I have to study all of the time."

"That isn't true," said Ms. Hernandez. "Here are some things I want you to remember!"

- Studying all of the time does not make you smarter! Your brain can only learn so much at once. Would you just eat and eat all day long? Probably not! After a while, your stomach just can't take any more food. The same is true for your brain. Your brain needs to rest, too!

- If you set up a study time, and work hard, then it's OK to play or to do other things the rest of the time. If you learn good study skills, you can be a "superhero" student. You can get more done in 30 minutes than most kids can get done in two hours! Ask your teacher or parent for study skills help.

- Remember that you are a kid! School is important, but playing, having fun, and being with your friends and family are important parts of growing up. Having fun does not mean that you will not do well on tests.

Set Up a Study Schedule

Instead of worrying about studying, set up a study schedule and follow it! If you study when you are supposed to, then you can have fun and you do not have to worry. Look at the "Sample Study Schedule" and then set up your own schedule.

Sample Study Schedule						
Sunday	**Monday**	**Tuesday**	**Wednesday**	**Thursday**	**Friday**	**Saturday**
fun time	3:30-4 p.m. video games	3:30-5 p.m. soccer	3:30-4 p.m. video games	3:30-5 p.m. soccer	3:30-4 p.m. video games	10 a.m. soccer game
fun time	4-4:30 p.m. review notes	5 p.m. dinner	4-4:30 p.m. review notes	5 p.m. dinner	4-4:30 p.m. review notes	12 p.m. team lunch
5 p.m. dinner	5 p.m. dinner	6-7 p.m. homework	5 p.m. dinner	6-7 p.m. homework	5 p.m. dinner	fun time
6-6:30 p.m. review notes	6-7 p.m. homework	7-7:30 p.m. review notes	6-7 p.m. homework	7-7:30 p.m. review notes	6-7 p.m. homework	fun time
6:30-7:30 homework	7-9 p.m. TV!	8-9 p.m. TV!	7-9 p.m. TV!	8-9 p.m. TV!	7-10 p.m. family time	fun time
	9 p.m. bedtime	9 p.m. bedtime	9 p.m. bedtime	9 p.m. bedtime	10 p.m. bedtime	

My Study Schedule						
Sunday	**Monday**	**Tuesday**	**Wednesday**	**Thursday**	**Friday**	**Saturday**

Activity 4

Be a Test-Taking Super Power! Don't Be a Victim Like Vince!

Vince was a nice kid, but when a test was coming up, he would be in a bad mood. He thought that tests were made just to ruin his life and that there was nothing he could do to make things better. Even worse, he thought that if he did not do well on a test, his poor grade was somebody else's fault! He would complain, "How could I do well on that test? My little brother ran around the apartment and made noise when I tried to study. It's his fault that I can't do well. And my mom didn't buy my favorite study snack, so how am I supposed to do my best? It is her fault, too!"

Vince's aunt was tired of his bad mood and all the complaining. "Vince," she said, "you are the one who is responsible for making sure that you do your best on tests. You have to have power over tests, not blame everyone else." Vince crossed his arms and made a mean face.

"Vince! Stop it right now and listen! Here is what you have to do!"

Vince's aunt took Vince by the arm and walked him around the apartment where he lived. "Where is a good place for you to study?"

"I don't know," said Vince.

"Well," said his aunt, "studying here in the kitchen is too noisy. Let's make a study place in your bedroom." Vince's aunt found an extra kitchen chair and a fold-up table. She set it up in the corner of Vince's bedroom. "Here you go, Vince," she said. "Now you can shut your door and have some quiet."

"And what about my snack?" asked Vince.

"Come to my house tomorrow. I need help packing up some old clothes. If you help me carry the boxes to my car, I will get you snacks for a month." Vince began to smile.

"Maybe I can be the boss of my studying," he thought.

If you study for tests in a place that helps you learn, you will have a better chance to show what you know. Look at where you study and ask yourself these questions!

- **Am I sitting at a table?** Most of the time, students learn best when they are sitting in chairs and are working at tables. You might be able to read a book while lying on the couch, but you should do most of your work at a table.

- **Do I have my study supplies near me?** You might want to have your textbook and study sheets on the table. You might also need a pen or pencil, a calculator, and other supplies. If they aren't near you, then you will have to get up and get them. This wastes study time and makes you forget what you learned.

- **Do I have enough light to see my work?** If there isn't enough light, your eyes will get tired. If your eyes get tired, you will get tired. That will be the end of studying!

- **Have I told people not to bother me?** Sometimes parents forget that they are making noise. They might also forget to tell your brothers and sisters to be quiet. Set a time to study and ask your family not to bother you during that time.

- **Am I hungry?** Most kids need an afternoon snack. It is hard to study if you are hungry.

- **Am I comfortable?** How does your chair feel? Is the table too high or too low? You might want to sit on a pillow or put one behind your back if your chair is hard or too low.

In the space below, write or draw how you might take control of where you study. Think about all the questions listed above.

I can take control of where I study! Here's how I'm going to do it.

Activity 5

Staying Away Won't Make Tests Go Away: The Story of "Stay-Away Stephanie"!

When Stephanie thought about tests, the first thing that came to her mind was to run away from them! Stephanie would do anything to not take a test. Once she pretended she was sick so she could stay home. Another time she asked the teacher for a pass to go to the restroom, and she never came back! These were not good choices. The test never went away! And Stephanie got in trouble with her mom and her teacher.

Stephanie's mom and teacher had a meeting with Stephanie. "Why do tests scare you so much?" they asked.

Stephanie replied, "Well, they are HUGE! I get so scared when I think about answering all those questions at once. I just want to forget about it!"

"Stephanie, your mom and I have a plan," said her teacher. "For the next few weeks, I am going to divide up one big test into a few smaller tests. Some tests will only have two or three questions on them. Practice taking those shorter tests and see how you feel. Then you can try some longer tests."

Stephanie didn't believe that the plan would work, but she was polite and said that she would try.

Stephanie's teacher took a big science test and divided it into 10 sections. Stephanie would do a section every day. Each section would get bigger and bigger as Stephanie had more test-taking practice. Look at Stephanie's plan on the top of the next page.

Guess what happened? Stephanie showed everything she knew on the science test. She decided she wouldn't stay away from tests anymore. "None of these questions are so bad. I can do a bunch all at once. I can be a good test taker like my friends. No more running away for me!"

Stephanie's Plan

- DAY 1: Do questions 1 and 2 ... finish 2 questions

- DAY 2: Do questions 3 and 4 ... finish 2 questions

- DAY 3: Do questions 5, 6, and 7 ... finish 3 questions

- DAY 4: Do questions 8, 9, and 10 ... finish 3 questions

- DAY 5: Do questions 11 through 14 ... finish 4 questions

- DAY 6: Do questions 15 through 19 ... finish 5 questions

- DAY 7: Do questions 20 through 27 ... finish 8 questions

- DAY 8: Do questions 28 through 37 ... finish 10 questions

- DAY 9: Do questions 38 through 50 ... finish 13 questions

- DAY 10: Yahoo! Test finished!

In the word search below, find words that describe things that sometimes scare kids (and grownups, too!). Can you find them all?

Tests	Monsters	Worms	Heights
Storms	Aliens	Bullies	Grizzlies
Spiders	Tornadoes	Lightning	School
Snakes	Robbers	Lizards	Bats

```
S N M O N S T E R S Q W E S T H G I E H
G R I Z Z L I E S R F N M E R T A W W P
X A D F G J B U L L I E S K I Y U A O B
V D I H Y Y T E S T S C I A L L P O R P
B A D I C U D R X A T T H N C D M J M S
N L G G Y A E O A B A S P S T O R M S C
L I Z A R D S G J K Q E R H J E M J Q H
O E B N I C G T O R N A D O E S B V T O
L N Q P X C O P J L I G H T N I N G V O
Q S S R E B B B O R E W G L U K S T A B L
```

I can be a test hero! Here's how I am going to do it!

☐ When I worry about tests, I will talk to someone about my feelings.

☐ I understand that tests are a chance for me to show what I know.

☐ I know that I can think good thoughts or bad thoughts, but I will choose to think good thoughts.

☐ I will set up a study schedule. I will study, but I will also give myself time to have fun.

☐ I will take control of my study habits, and I will succeed!

☐ I won't stay away from tests.

Chapter 2

Getting Rid of Test Stress

In this chapter, you are going to learn about test stress, a yucky feeling that some people have around test time. You may find that you have a little or a lot of test stress. If you do, that is OK. Use what you learn from each of these activities to help you feel better about taking tests. You will soon be a super test taker!

In This Chapter . . .

Activity 6

Beat the Test Monster by Being Calm! It Sounds Crazy, but It Works!

You might not know it, but there is a test monster waiting to make sure that you mess up when you take a test. No one knows why he behaves so badly, but he does!

The test monster tries to bother students in a lot of ways. This makes the test monster laugh and makes kids upset!

One of his tricks is to make your body feel so yucky that you can't think clearly about all that you know. The test monster can make your heart pound like a drum. He can make your hands sweat or shake. Sometimes, the test monster makes your stomach hurt. He is sure that if you don't feel well (if you are stressed), you won't do your best on the test!

If the test monster bothers you, there are ways to fight back. But this doesn't mean that you should hit him on the head! The best idea is to be so calm that he can't bother you. If you learn to relax your body, the test monster will give up and leave you alone. Learning how to relax is easy.

When your body feels stressed, find a comfortable chair and sit down. Or, in school, stretch out in your chair. Close your eyes and breathe very slowly. Count to four while you breathe in and then count to four when you breathe out. Do this five to 10 times. While you are breathing very slowly, chase the test monster away by thinking of something really nice or fun. Because all kids are different, there are many different things that kids think about to relax. Some might think of their favorite foods. Another kid might think about the best cartoon he or she has ever seen or playing with a special pet.

If the test monster visits, what happy thoughts could you think about? List some ideas below! Think happy thoughts to get rid of the test monster.

My Happy Thoughts

1. _____

   _____

2. _____

   _____

3. _____

   _____

4. _____

   _____

5. _____

   _____

Activity 7

The Test Monster Strikes Again!

Hey, weren't we supposed to have said goodbye to that test monster? Well, he still has more tricks up his sleeve!

Even if you chase the test monster away by being calm and thinking happy thoughts, he still has other ways to stop you from doing your best on tests. One of his meanest weapons is to make you think that you can't do anything right. Even the smartest kids get fooled by the test monster. They start thinking that they will fail. They don't see good things about themselves. When they feel this way it makes tests seem too hard. They give up or make silly mistakes. The test monster can make you believe that nothing you do is right.

The best news is that the test monster is wrong! All kids are wonderful, including YOU! You don't have to be the best student in your class to be special and successful. You just have to discover the great things about yourself.

All kids have "buried treasures" inside of them. When you find these treasures, the test monster can NEVER make you feel badly about yourself. Diego wrote down good things about himself. Look at his list. Because there are so many special things about Diego, the test monster can't make him feel badly.

Diego's Buried Treasures

1. I am the best dog trainer in my family.
2. No one makes better chocolate milk than me.
3. I read two whole chapters of my library book in one day.
4. I always pass my spelling tests!

In the spaces given, write down all the good things about yourself that you can think of. If it is hard to begin, ask a parent, a friend, or a teacher to help. Not every special thing about you has to do with school. There will be many wonderful things to say about you because you are special.

After you have completed "My Buried Treasures," look at all the wonderful things about yourself. You have many treasures inside of you. Now, if you are this special, you know that you can do your best on tests! The test monster will never be able to get you down.

My Buried Treasures

1. _____

2. _____

3. _____

4. _____

5. _____

6. _____

7. _____

8. _____

Activity 8

Don't Think Like a Fool and You Won't be a Failure at School

Bud's life was going just fine until the day he slipped at the pool. Now, since he didn't get hurt, it seems rather silly that a little slip could ruin his life, but that is exactly what happened, at least for a while. And here is the story!

Bud and his friends loved going to the town pool. It was a great way to enjoy a summer afternoon and to see all the kids from school. The town pool had two slides. The pool also had something that looked like a mushroom with water squirting out, and little kids could play under it. The pool also had two diving boards at the deep end. There were picnic tables, a snack bar, and a recreation room with a Ping-Pong table and a basketball hoop. Until that fateful day, Bud felt comfortable when he spent time at the pool.

Then the big slip happened. It really wasn't a big slip, but it felt that way to Bud. As a matter of fact, it felt bigger and bigger every time Bud thought about it. Bud was climbing up the stairs to the tallest diving board when his feet slipped out from under him. Luckily, he grabbed the handrails and steadied himself. He didn't even get a scratch, but he was scared, really scared. He thought about what would happen if he had fallen on the hard concrete below. Then his friends started teasing him about being "clumsy." They didn't mean to hurt his feelings, but they did.

Bud couldn't get this out of his mind. Over the next few weeks, he began to think that he was not coordinated enough to do anything. He began to miss hits in baseball, and he wouldn't jump on the trampoline at home. He also started thinking that his ability to do other things wasn't very good either. He started getting very nervous about tests and school. He started to not like himself very much.

When the school year began, Bud's mother took him to the school counselor. Ms. Schubert knew exactly what was happening to Bud. "Looks like a serious case of generalization here!" she exclaimed. "Bud, your brain is playing tricks on you. You had one bad thing happen, and now you think that things are bad in general. But that's not true. You are still the same wonderful Bud that I have known since you were in kindergarten! Just because you had one bad experience doesn't mean that everything will turn out badly."

This made sense to Bud. "You know, it was just a little slip at the pool. I still have all the talents that make me special!"

"You are right," said his mother happily. When they got home, she reminded Bud of things he had done well. She asked him to tell her why these things were important. "This is where I won an award for attendance! I can be responsible! And here is a certificate for entering my model car in a race. I do a good job of building and painting model cars, and that takes coordination! And, best of all, I did it myself!" Now Bud was feeling better.

Sometimes when kids have a hard time on a test, a project, or an assignment, they start feeling badly about themselves, too. They forget all that they have done in their lives and all the skills and talents that they have. That one bad experience starts to ruin everything! They tell themselves, "I am generally not a very good student." Once they start that kind of thinking, life is only going to get worse!

We all have done great stuff in our lives, but sometimes we forget about it. Just as Bud's mom showed him things that reminded him of all he could do, you should do the same for yourself! Find five photographs, certificates, or other things that will help you remember the past. Lay them out on a table and have a parent or another adult help you remember good things about yourself. What were you doing in the photo? How did you earn the certificate? What did you do in those old baseball shoes?

Then make a chart like the one below. Write down what item you were looking at, what happened, and what you learned about yourself by talking about it. Bud filled in the first row of the chart to give you a head start!

Item	What Happened	What I Learned About Me
Model car	I built it by myself.	I can be successful on my own.
_____	_____	_____
_____	_____	_____
_____	_____	_____
_____	_____	_____

If you fill out this chart, you will not let yourself be fooled by a mistake or two. Instead, you will show what you know and know all that you can do!

Activity 9

Your Worries Will SHRINk If You Share What You Think

Randy and Jimmy were young brothers who had a special talent. They lived on a big ranch, and ever since they could remember they had been riding horses. Some of the time they rode to help their father check to see if the fences around their ranch were standing, and other times they rode to see if they could find a lost cow. But the most fun they had was riding in the "Wild West" parade that happened every summer in the nearest town. Randy and Jeff would dress up in their finest riding clothes and would wear big black cowboy hats that their grandfather bought them. They had special saddles for their horses. They also had state flags on tall poles that they carried as they rode.

One winter day Randy was bored. He had no homework to do, no new library books to read, and it was much too cold to go out and play. So Randy went to the barn to explore. He played with the barn cats and pretended to ride a tractor. Soon he laid eyes on the clothes, flags, and saddles that he and Jimmy used in the "Wild West" parade. "This looks like fun," thought Randy. "I will bring this saddle up in the hayloft and the other stuff too. I will pretend that I am riding on a hot summer day."

Randy took the saddle up to the hayloft. He lifted his hat into the air. He bounced up and down, imagining how everyone in town thought he was the best rider ever. Suddenly, he lost his balance. He didn't fall out of the hayloft, but the flags and his hat fell to the floor below. His hat was covered with mud and both flagpoles were broken. Randy was scared and ashamed. He just wanted to forget about it all and never tell anyone. So he hid the hat and the poles behind some extra pieces of lumber and went back into the house.

But of course the story didn't end there! First of all, his problem didn't go away. The hat was still a mess and the poles were too. Second, the more time that went by, the worse Randy felt. Third, the more he kept his worries inside, the BIGGER they got! Randy's thoughts went as wild as the parade!

Here is what Randy thought:

- I am going to be in the biggest trouble ever. My life will be ruined.
- Jimmy will be so angry that he will not want to be my brother.
- I'll never get a hat as nice as the one I messed up.
- There is no way I will ever ride in the "Wild West" parade again.
- I am the dumbest kid in the world.

A few weeks later, Randy's father went to the barn to do some work. And guess what he found? The dirty hat and the broken poles. Because he was a good kid, Randy told his dad the truth about what happened, but he was crying so hard that his father could hardly understand what Randy was saying. Finally, after Randy calmed down a little, he and his father sat down and talked. Can you guess what Randy found out? He found out that his thoughts were wrong!

Randy's dad told him that there were a lot of things a kid could do that were worse than this mistake. He told him that he had to be punished for not telling sooner, but that doing a few extra chores was not going to ruin his life. Randy was beginning to feel better.

Jimmy wasn't angry. In fact, he told Randy that he went to the barn and ran around with the flags a couple days before Randy dropped them. He made mistakes too. After the brothers talked, they started laughing about riding a fake horse. And they got along fine after that.

Randy had $66 in the bank, and he got $5 a week for an allowance from his parents. A new hat cost $90. Every week, Randy saved $3 and put it in his "hat bank." In a couple of months (way before summer!), Randy had enough money to buy a new hat.

Randy and Jimmy rode in the parade after all. They didn't have the flags, but they waved at everyone and got to throw candy to little kids who watched from the street.

By saving his money and thinking about what he would do differently next time, Randy found out that he sure wasn't a dumb kid!

You may think, "What does this have to do with taking tests?" Lots of students have scary thoughts about school and tests. That is a problem, but the problem gets worse when they don't talk about their worried feelings. Then their worries get bigger and bigger and scarier and scarier. Soon they feel a lot like Randy!

Take a look at these stories. Each story is about a kid who is very worried about school. All the kids think that the worst will happen! Make believe that they talked to you about their fears. Help them feel better by writing what they can do to help themselves and what really might happen (which isn't as bad as they think).

Look at this first example; then you can do the rest!

1. Shankra lost her test-taking book the week before the big test. "My teacher will be so mad at me!" thought Shankra. "And my parents expect me to be perfect on the test. Because I made this one mistake, I will fail for sure!"

   What could Shankra do to help herself? _Shankra could ask the teacher for a new book, or she could borrow a friend's book. She could tell herself that everyone makes mistakes. She could think about all that she studied and learned before she lost the book._

   What really might happen? _Shankra's teacher won't be mad, just a little bothered. Shankra's parents will understand but will expect her to try to be more responsible next time. Shankra will not fail the test because she is a hard-working student who has learned a lot all year. She might even do really well on the big test!_

Now, here are some other stories!

2. Ted was good at a lot of things, but he wasn't very good at math. He would look around at his classmates and think to himself, "They are so much better than me. I don't like myself very much." Ted would not do his math homework because he thought, "I know I will never learn it, so why bother?" Ted would get very upset thinking about his brother who was in middle school, "I will be the worst math student ever by that time!"

What could Ted do to help himself?

_____

_____

_____

_____

What really might happen?

_____

_____

_____

_____

3. April was very, very nervous about taking tests. All she could think about was the chance that she would be so sick to her stomach that she would have to run to the girl's room during the test. If she found one question to be a little hard, she thought, "Well, it is over for me!" April figured that she would be left behind in her grade. "I will never have a very happy life as long as I have to go to school," she thought.

What could April do to help herself?

_____

_____

_____

_____

What really might happen?

_____

_____

_____

_____

Teach Your Body to be the Boss of Your Brain and Your Worries About Tests Will Go Down the Drain!

It's good that you have a brain, especially because your brain is your friend. But like your friends, a brain can be a bother at times, even if it means to be helpful. When you think of your brain, you usually think about solving problems and learning, but your brain does much more. One of the biggest jobs your brain has is to protect you from harm. You could think of your brain as your own police officer! And your brain does this in two ways. One, it makes you think about what you should do to be safe. Two, it gives signals to your body when something is wrong, kind of like a fire alarm!

Sometimes your brain protects you by making you feel guilty or scared. Then your thoughts make you feel badly about what you did or tell you to get away! But to make sure you learn your lesson and do better next time, your brain might make your stomach hurt a little or your heart beat faster.

Clark lived just a couple blocks away from a factory where cars were made. He could look through the fence to try to see what was going on at the factory, but he couldn't see much. His mother told him over and over again not to go beyond the fence because that was "restricted" property ("restricted" means that only certain people can enter). But one day, after a big rainstorm, Clark saw a hole in the fence and climbed through. As he was walking toward the buildings where the cars were made, a security guard stopped him and sternly told him NEVER to come back. "Do you know that our machines pour metal that is as hot as a volcano?" barked the guard. "When our delivery trucks back up, they can't see a kid standing there. Now do you see why you can't be here?"

Clark felt embarrassed about his behavior. He also felt scared. His heart was racing. "I will never do that again," thought Clark. That was a good thing because, unless you know what you are doing, it is too dangerous to go into a big factory and explore. You could get hurt by machines or run over by trucks. "I should have listened to my mother." Clark's brain was protecting him.

But sometimes your brain can do too good of a job at protecting you. When it should nicely tell you "be careful" or "pay attention," instead it screams, "The most terrible thing is happening!" Then your body gets out of control. You can't stop thinking of all the bad things that could happen. Your heart feels like it is going to explode and your head hurts. Your stomach doesn't feel too well either. You feel like you can't breathe. The worse your body feels, the more you think about problems. And the more you worry and panic, the worse your body feels. It is like being trapped on a roller coaster that never stops!

A fifth grader named Garrett worried a lot about schoolwork and tests. His brain thought that it was doing a great job of protecting Garrett, but his brain was wrong. Instead of telling Garrett, "You better pay attention to your lessons so you will do your best on the test," Garrett's brain yelled, "That test is out to get you! It is going to be like the scariest movie you ever saw! You better forget about doing a good job!" Right away, Garrett felt like there was a hundred-pound weight on his chest. He could hardly breathe. His head was pounding. That only reminded him of how bad things were, and then he felt even worse.

One day in math class, Mr. Donatello announced that there was going to be a test on long division. Now Garrett was a good kid, but he wasn't great at doing division. Before you could say "12 divided by two equals six," his brain was at work, telling him that a bad thing was going to happen, and his started feeling sick to his stomach. Mr. Donatello saw that Garrett was upset. He took him aside and drew him this picture:

"Garrett," said Mr. Donatello, "you have to get control of yourself. One way to do this is to teach your body to ignore your brain."

"But," replied Garrett, "you teachers always tell us never to ignore stuff!"

"This is different," said Mr. Donatello. "When your brain makes your body upset, you have to get back in control by not paying attention to what your brain is saying. When your body feels better, you will feel better and the upsetting thoughts will go away."

Mr. Donatello gave Garret a little book with some drawings in it. They looked like this:

Breathe in and hold your breath for a second or two.

Blow out slowly.

While you breathe in and out, stretch your legs and then let them relax.

Now keep breathing and stretch your arms and let them relax.

Make a tight fist and then let it relax. Remember to breathe slowly in and out.

If no one is looking, squeeze your face and then let it relax.

"If you practice these exercises, you can control your body," said Mr. Donatello. "It might sound a little silly, but it works. I used them when I was in college. They helped me get through some really hard tests!"

In the space below, draw a picture of how you would make your body the boss of your brain! You can use the ideas that Mr. Donatello taught Garrett, or you can come up with ideas of your own. For example, Garrett decided that it would help to squeeze his baseball, and his idea worked great! Then, in the space below the picture, write a few sentences about what was worrying you and what you did to help yourself.

I can make my body the boss of my brain!

Activity 11

Be Your Own Cheerleader!

Shannon loved almost everything about her school, Winding Brook Elementary. She cared about her friends, liked her teachers, and always wanted her school to be the best. That is why she decided to be a cheerleader for the Winding Brook Elementary "Bobcats" football team. Shannon wanted to do everything that she could to help the Bobcats do their best, so she joined the cheerleading team. There were four girls and four boys on the team, and it was an honor to be chosen. You had to know how to dance (at least a little) and do some flips and somersaults. Yelling loudly was also a good thing!

One day the Bobcats were having a very hard game. Their luck was terrible! They dropped balls when they tried to catch passes, slipped when they ran, and got tackled all the time. At halftime, they were behind by a score of 28 to 7. Shannon and her cheerleading teammates were worried. Although they were singing the school pride song and were cheering with the crowd, nothing was working. Instead, the kids on the football team looked sadder and sadder and made more and more mistakes.

Suddenly, Shannon had an idea. "We need to cheer for EVERYTHING that those kids do right, not just if they score. We need to remind them of how good they are!" Shannon went on, "We will watch all the kids on the team. If they do something well, then we will give them their own little cheer. Like if Matt makes even a very small run, we will cheer him on by saying something like 'Hey Matt! Way to run! You make football great and fun!' We will show them all the good they can do. That might make them feel better and have fewer mistakes."

When halftime was over, Shannon and the other cheerleaders followed Shannon's idea. They paid attention to every good thing that the football players did. At first, the players were surprised and so were the people watching the game. But then, after a few minutes, things began to change. The more Shannon and the cheerleaders cheered for even little good things, the better the Bobcats did! At the end of the game, the Bobcats lost, but the score was much closer, 31 to 28. And although they lost the game, the whole school learned something wonderful, thanks to Shannon and her friends! They learned that you have to keep paying attention to what you can do, not what is causing you trouble.

When it comes to schoolwork and tests, cheerleading works too! Now it isn't likely that every classroom will have its own cheerleader, but you can be your own cheerleader! To do that, you have to do two things!

- Pay attention to what you do well, and make what you do well more important than worrying about your mistakes. If you are having a hard time finishing a book report, think about all you have already done. "I read the book, I wrote the first paragraph of the report, and I know what picture I want to draw to illustrate my report."

- Cheer yourself on! For everything that you do, give yourself a little cheer. You might want to say to yourself, "I'm halfway there, I'm pretty smart, I know I can do the other part!" You don't have to make a rhyme or cheer every time (even though it is fun to do), but you can say things like, "I did two problems correctly, good for me and my brain!" or "I am proud of myself for reading four chapters, even if I have three more to go." You can also say simple things like, "Good job so far!" or "Look at all I did in 10 minutes." Even "Super" or "I can do this" works fine! You can also cheer for paying attention, being polite, trying hard, learning something new, figuring out a problem, or getting your desk better organized!

Think about a day in school. What could you have said to yourself to cheer yourself on? Here is what a third grader named Abu wrote about his day.

Got up in the morning. I remembered to bring a red pen to school like my teacher told us yesterday. Great job! My memory is getting better. I feel a little more like a grownup.

Went on the bus. I said "Hello" to Mr. Weaver, the bus driver, and he smiled. I thought, "I can be a friendly kid . . . good for me!" This made me smile too.

At school we had reading. I read six new words out of 10 correctly. I told myself, "Great job, you got more than half of them right!" I knew that I had to study more, but I was proud of what I could do. Reading is a little hard for me, but I feel like I can do it.

Then we had to work on our science projects. My glue wasn't sticking to the dinosaur I was building, but I was able to put on a few fake bones. I told myself, "I had a problem and I fixed it." That was a lot better than telling myself that I wasn't building the dinosaur as fast as I wanted to.

When we had physical education, I was the fourth fastest in the 100-yard dash. I told myself, "You're pretty quick!" I didn't spend much time thinking about the kids who were faster. I was just proud of myself.

When I got home I had to ask my mom for a lot of homework help. I told myself, "I've got the good sense to ask for help." I didn't get down on myself for not knowing everything. I didn't feel frustrated and I was glad that my mom is so smart!

Look at the chart below. Think about what you did during a school day and try to be your own cheerleader. Write down something great that you did, describe how you cheered for yourself, and how you felt.

What I Did that Was Great	What I Did to be My Own Cheerleader	How It Made Me Feel

Activity 12

Be a Winner! Get Everyone on Your Team!

If you've never heard of a "Fast Facts" contest, then you probably aren't alone. Steven didn't have the slightest idea of what a "Fast Facts" contest was either, until Mr. Cooper came to school. Mr. Cooper was the owner of a big grocery store. Steven's father said that Mr. Cooper and his family were 'good people.' "They always try to make our town a better place," said Steven's father. Mr. Cooper had a idea that would help raise enough money to buy a new computer for the school library and build a bike trail around the school. What was that idea? Everyone in school would join a "Fast Facts" contest. Mr. Cooper promised that the harder kids worked, the more money he would give the school to help them get the computer and bike trail.

Steven listened closely as Mr. Cooper told of his plan. "At the end of the school day next Tuesday, every student will be given a list of 100 questions to answer. Every kid will get a different list. There will be all kinds of questions, and you will have to find answers in different ways. And, most importantly, you can get help to find the answers. It is your responsibility to figure out how to get the best help so you can answer as many questions correctly by the start of school on Wednesday. I will give the school one dollar for every correct answer."

Steven was very excited when he received his list on Tuesday afternoon. He tore open the envelope and his eyes ran up and down the list of questions. Soon, he was coming up with a plan!

The first part of his plan was to get home as quickly as he could because he knew that help was there! He had a mother, a father, and an older brother. He also had a little sister, but he wasn't sure if she was a help or a bother! He also had a computer and books. He probably had other things that could help, but he would find that out as the contest went on!

Steven got pens of different colors and began to make marks on the list. He used a red pen to mark questions that he probably could find on the computer or in books. These were questions like, "What is the capital of Mexico?" or "How many bees does it take to make a pound of honey?" There were other questions that needed something to be done. "How many statues of soldiers do we have in our town?" He marked these with a green pen. To find that out, Steven knew he needed to ask someone who either drove around a lot or lived in the town for a long time and knew the answer. Or he had to ask someone to take a trip around town and count the statues! One question asked, "Draw a picture of where the moon is in the sky tonight." Someone was going to have to go out and see and then make a quick drawing.

As time went by, Steven learned that he could get all kinds of help. Pretty soon, he had a big team of "Fast Fact" finders. His older brother was quick with the computer and kept running up to his room to look up answers while Steven stayed downstairs doing other things. Steven's dad became the "do it all" guy. He went to the courthouse and counted the number of bricks on the old steps. Then he went to the store to find out how many grams of sugar were in a chocolate bar. Steven's mother worked hard too. She helped Steven figure out some math problems on the calculator and looked up some weird words in the dictionary. Steven found out that "massive" meant "huge"! (Now Steven knows to ask for a "massive" piece of pie for dessert!) Steven also went next door and asked Mrs. Ruskin for help with history. She was an older lady, but she acted fun and young! She knew the answer right away! He also called his uncle, who was a doctor, and he knew all about how people catch colds. And Steven's little sister helped too! She stayed nice and quiet, playing on the rug while everyone was working. She even gave Steven a messy and drooly cookie that she was eating! Steven did a lot of the fact finding too, and he worked very, very hard!

When he finally went to bed that night, Steven had learned a lot of important things. First, he knew he could work hard to reach a goal. He also learned a whole bunch of facts, more than he had ever learned before. But mostly, he now knew that he needed a team to do well! "It's much better to ask for help," thought Steven as he climbed into bed. "Now I will be sure to ask for help when I need it. If I have to do homework or a project, or have to study for a test, I know it is always good to ask for help. I won't ask all the time (Steven didn't want to be like his baby sister!), but I will ask when I need it. This is how I will do my best!"

You can also find a team to help you show what you know and be a school and test-taking star! Make a list of all the people who can be on your team and how they can help you. You can also put on that list what tools you have to help you do your best. The list on the next page shows how one student, Anise, got others to help her. The list also shows things Anise used to show what she knows.

Who or What Can Help Me	How They Can Help
My mom	She knows spelling very well and can drive me to the library.
My dad	He is great at math; he calms me down if I'm upset.
My sister Kayla	She is a good artist, and she went to my school when she was in my grade and knows what I should study.
Books at home	We have an atlas and a huge dictionary.
Computer	I can look up facts and practice my writing.
Bicycle	I can ride to the library.
Mrs. Franks	She's a teacher and lives down the street.
My teacher	She lets kids come in early and get extra help.

Now it's time for you to make your own team! Fill in the list below and see how you can get help to show what you know!

Who or What Can Help Me	How They Can Help
_____	_____
_____	_____
_____	_____
_____	_____
_____	_____
_____	_____

I can get rid of test stress! Here's how I am going to do it!

☐ I will beat the test monster by staying calm.

☐ I know that I have many treasures inside of me, and I won't let the test monster get me down.

☐ Even though I sometimes make mistakes, I will remember that I am special and that I can do my best in school.

☐ I will share my worries with others.

☐ I will be the boss of my brain.

☐ I will be a cheerleader for myself and others.

☐ If I ask others to help me, I will do my best.

Chapter 3

How Do You Learn?

In this chapter, you are going to find out different ways that people learn. When you know how you learn, you will be better prepared to do well on tests.

In This Chapter . . .

Activity 13

Take This Test to Find Out How You Learn Best!

Olivia loved ballet! She begged her mother to let her take lessons. And, after her lessons, she practiced and practiced to do her best. She loved to dance in front of the big mirror in the dining room. She imagined that she was dancing in front of hundreds of people who were all clapping for her. Because Olivia worked so hard, you would think that learning new dance steps would not be a problem for her. But it was! She learned everything slowly and she couldn't figure out why. Her teacher would tell her what to do, but she was always the last one to learn.

One day Olivia's ballet teacher spent time with Olivia after class. She showed Olivia what to do. Olivia watched carefully. The teacher pointed her toes down as her hands went up. The teacher looked up at the ceiling as she jumped.

Suddenly, Olivia understood! She got up and danced like she never had danced before!

Olivia found out that she learns best when she is SEEING the lesson. That is different from some people who learn by HEARING or others who learn by DOING.

Olivia learns by SEEING. When she sees her teacher dance, she understands.

Kara learns by HEARING. When she hears her teacher talking, she understands the subject.

Kyle learns by DOING. When he does a few addition problems, he begins to understand how to add.

Take the test below. It will help you find out how you learn best. For each question, circle the answer that is most like you!

1. You and your friends go to a scary movie. After the movie, your parents take you out for ice cream. You tell your parents all about the movie. What do you remember the most?

   a. What everyone said and the terrible noises that the monster made

   b. How horrible the monster looked

   c. Your scary feelings during the movie

2. Your best friend has not been very nice to you. In fact, your friend won't sit with you anymore. What do you do to solve this problem?

   a. You talk to another friend and your mother.

   b. You remember all the ways that you are a good friend to remind yourself that this isn't your fault.

   c. You take your dog for a walk and try to calm down and forget about it.

3. You are at the mall with your dad and your sister. Your dad tells you that the car is parked in garage number four and in row eight. He wants you and your sister to meet him there in 10 minutes. You don't have a pen or any paper. How do you remember where the car is parked?

   a. You repeat "garage four, row eight" over and over until you find the car.

   b. You imagine a sign that says "garage four, row eight" in your mind.

   c. You "write" the information on your hand with your finger.

4. It is time for the big math test. Every kid in your grade is supposed to take the test, but there is a big problem! The heater breaks and everyone has to take the test in the gym. What would bother you the most when you are taking your test?

   a. People making noises in the hallway and in the lunchroom

   b. Seeing your friends from other classes who are also in the gym

   c. Being cold, even with your coat on

5. Your family has a big holiday party every year. A lot of the same people come back every year. How do you remember whether you have met them before?

    a. You usually remember their names.

    b. You remember seeing their faces before.

    c. You remember something about them, like the way they speak or how they act.

6. Your favorite clothes are:

    a. Whatever fits and looks OK.

    b. Always your favorite color.

    c. Very comfortable so you can move around easily.

7. One day you fall off your bike and break your leg. You have to stay in bed for four weeks. How do you spend a lot of your time?

    a. Talk to your friends on the phone and call your grandmother every day

    b. Watch videos

    c. Do some crafts and exercise the best that you can

8. Your school is getting ready for "Spirit Week." Your class is in charge of decorating the halls. The principal comes to your room to give everyone directions. What do you do while the principal is talking?

    a. Listen very carefully

    b. Try to sit near the front of the group and watch the principal closely

    c. Imagine what your class will do to get ready for "Spirit Week"

9. While you are working on a book report about trains, your older brother tells you that the way you spelled "locomotive" is wrong. If you don't have a spell checker, how do you know if your brother could be right?

    a. You sound out the word, syllable by syllable.

    b. You try to picture in your mind what that word looked like in a book you just read called "Trains of the Old West."

    c. You write the word in a bunch of different ways and see which one looks correct.

10. It is your birthday and your aunt wants to do something special with you. She suggests going to hear the college band play, going to a museum, or trying out a climbing wall. All those ideas sound fun, but which would you most likely choose?

a. The college band concert

b. A trip to a museum

c. The climbing wall

NOW, SCORE YOUR TEST! Count the number of "a," "b," and "c" answers and put the totals below.

Number of "a" answers _____

Number of "b" answers _____

Number of "c" answers _____

HERE IS WHAT YOUR SCORES MEAN!

- If most of your answers were "a," then you learn best by HEARING.

- If most of your answers were "b," then you learn best by SEEING.

- If most of your answers were "c," then you learn best by DOING.

Go over this test with your parents and teachers. See if they have some good ideas to help you learn in your own special way!

Activity 14

Seeing Learners, Hearing Learners, Doing Learners . . . Everyone Has a Special Way to Take a Test!

In the previous activity, you took a test to help you better understand what type of "learner" you are. Some kids learn better when they SEE what they are learning, some kids do better when they HEAR what they are learning, and some kids do better when they are DOING something as they learn. Most students learn in many different ways, but for most of us, some ways are better than others. Because of this, different people need different tools to do their best on tests.

If you are a **SEEING** learner, here are some ideas to help you be a test hero.

- Make sure that you circle or underline important words in test questions and answers.
- Drawing a picture could help you remember what to write about or it could help you solve a problem.
- Don't watch television when studying for a test. No kid should do that anyway, but for SEEING learners, it really gets in the way of doing their best.
- Spend some time imagining what you will do on the day of the test and how you will use all the test skills you have learned.
- Draw a picture of yourself as a "test hero." Put it on your bedroom wall and look at it every night.

If you are a **HEARING** learner, here are some special ideas for you.

- Don't be afraid to talk to yourself! It sounds a little weird, but it works! Tell yourself that you will beat the test monster and you will do well on the test. Remind yourself of all the wonderful things you have learned.
- Say test directions quietly to yourself. Read them slowly and carefully.
- Make sure that you study in a quiet place or with a little music to make you calm.
- Ask your teacher if you can sit in a quiet place to take the test.

DOING learners also get some pretty cool ideas!

- Pay attention to your handwriting. DOING learners can get lazy with their handwriting, so take your time and make sure people can read what you write.
- Ask your teacher if you can sit in a place where you can stretch out or move a little during the test.
- Don't put down the first answer that comes in your mind. Spend a little time working out the problem on paper or rereading the question.
- Make sure that you dress in comfortable clothes on the test day.
- Check all your answers twice! DOING learners are active kids, and it is easy to make silly mistakes.

Here are some pictures of kids who learn differently. One is a SEEING learner, one is a HEARING learner, and one is, of course, a DOING learner. Can you label them correctly? Write your answers on the lines above the pictures.

Thanks for telling me to keep my eyes on the ball. I caught 2 tough passes!

Activity 15

An Active Brain Is a Happy Brain!

Darnell was not in a good mood. Here he was, standing in the middle of a big art museum with his mother and grandmother instead of being with his friends. "It's a nice sunny day out, and I could be riding my bike to the park with my buddies," thought Darnell. "But here I am, stuck inside listening to some old guy talk about a bunch of paintings." Darnell didn't complain out loud, but he hung his head and turned off his brain to what the guide was saying. "Just get me out of here!" he whispered to himself.

Suddenly, in spite of himself, Darnell heard the guide say, "The artist painted this picture while he was a prisoner in the Civil War."

Darnell thought to himself, "How in the world could a prisoner paint a picture? He would be all locked up and everything. That doesn't make sense to me." All of a sudden, Darnell found himself asking this question to his mother.

The guide heard his question and said, "That is a good question and here is the answer. The war had two sides. The warden of the prison gave this artist art supplies and ordered him to only paint what made the warden's side look good!" Now that really got Darnell thinking.

"Well," he asked the guide, looking right at him, "why didn't the prisoner just do a terrible job on purpose? That would serve the warden a lesson!"

"Young man," said the guide, "that would be one idea. But what this artist did was do the best that he could so that after the war was over, everyone could see that his side could never be broken down. Even in prison, he was able to do a great job. That really showed who was the best!"

All of a sudden, Darnell realized that he was learning about art. And, most surprising of all, it wasn't boring. He began to look at all the paintings around him and started asking himself questions. "How do painters make everything look so real? Some of these old paintings look like photographs. Why did they paint so many angels years ago?" Darnell began to open up his brain. He looked around him, listened to the guide, asked questions, and even shared ideas of his own. Before he knew it, he was an art expert. Darnell had become an active learner. And he was happy, even if he wasn't outside with his friends.

If you aren't an active learner, what you should be learning will go in one ear and out the other, never stopping in your brain. You will feel bored and unhappy in school. You might sit in your classroom every day, but if you are a "couch potato learner," you aren't using your brain!

Being an active learner takes time and practice. If you are usually bored in school, it is going to take some time to learn to be an active learner, but you can do it. You will be amazed at how much you will learn. You might even shock your brain. And everyone can do it!

Here are ways to be an active learner. How many of them do you do?

- Try to look at the teacher. You learn with your eyes and ears. What you see keeps you interested and gives you more information.

- Pay attention to what you are hearing. Tell yourself, "I need to listen to what the teacher is saying. If I do, I will learn more and feel better about myself and about school."

- Ask questions about the lesson. Don't just sit there and think, "Well, I guess I will figure this out someday." Raise your hand and ask what is on your mind. This will help you learn and remember.

- Think of your own ideas and share them with others. You might not be the teacher, but you have a good brain and lots of thoughts. Sharing your ideas helps you be a better student.

- Work with others. The more you talk about your schoolwork and solve problems with your classmates, the more everyone will learn.

- Don't be a "clock watcher." Instead of wondering, "When will this day be over?" think to yourself, "What else can I learn today?"

- Ask yourself, "Why am I learning this?" Instead of complaining, "This math is too hard and boring!" you should think about all the ways you can use math to help yourself now and later. "Division will help me divide up my baseball cards with my brothers."

- Go over your work with your parents or family members. This gives you another chance to ask questions and share ideas.

Now, check out how much you know about being an active learner. Are these statements true or false? Write a T for true or an F for false on the line given.

1. _____ You should always work by yourself when studying for a test.

2. _____ Watching the clock will make school go by faster.

3. _____ If you ask questions, it means you aren't a very good student.

4. _____ A lot of what we learn in school isn't very helpful.

5. _____ Looking at the floor when the teacher is talking helps us learn best.

6. _____ Don't think about your own ideas because the teacher knows everything.

7. _____ It only takes a day to become an active learner.

8. _____ If you just sit in class, what the teacher says will stay in your brain.

9. _____ There is nothing that you can do about being bored in school.

10. _____ Only the smartest kids can be active learners.

I will find out how I learn! Here's how I am going to do it!

☐ I will think about whether I am a seeing learner, a hearing learner, or a doing learner.

☐ I will use what I know about how I learn to do my best.

☐ I will keep my brain active.

Chapter 4

Make the Most of Your Study Time

In this chapter, you are going to learn how to use your study time wisely. When you make the most of your study time, you will be better prepared to do well on tests.

In This Chapter . . .

Activity 16

A Messy Room Doesn't Help and Neither Does a Messy Brain!

Your brain is full of knowledge, but sometimes it is hard to find where you put it all! That is because most of us haven't had practice making our brains neat and tidy. If we aren't careful, our brains can be like a really messy bedroom. If your bedroom is a disaster, you probably won't be able to find everything that you need. You might be able to find something here and there, but that's about all. If you had put things neatly away, you'd have what you needed in a second!

When you study for tests, it is helpful to try to figure out where to "store" that knowledge. If you do it right, you can find it any time you like. If you don't store it where you can find it, you'll search until you are tired out. What happens to your test scores then? They, too, are a mess!

Zach was getting ready for a science test. Zach thought to himself, "I'm going to make sure I know where to find what I need when I take the test." To do this, when Zach listened to the teacher or read his book, he thought about what "box" he should use to store that knowledge. On Monday and Tuesday, the class studied trees. They learned the parts of trees, the kinds of trees that grow in the United States, and what trees need to be healthy. Instead of mixing up all of that information in one box, Zach made three brain boxes. In one, he put all that he learned about the parts of trees. In the second, he added all that he knew about the kinds of trees in the United States. But Zach was even smarter than he thought! Zach divided his "Kinds of Trees" box into two different boxes! He labeled one "Colder Climate" for trees that survive in colder climates and another "Warm Climate" for trees that grow in warm climates. Then he made a third box about keeping trees healthy. When the test came, guess who got a great grade?

Parts of Trees	Kinds of Trees		Keeping Trees Healthy
	Colder Climate	**Warm Climate**	
trunk roots bark leaves branches	pine spruce fir	palm fruit trees	proper pruning enough water fertilizer good location prevent wounds

You can learn to find what you know quickly and without making yourself stressed. To practice, look at the words below. They should be placed in either the Transportation box, the Music box, or the Food box. Ask a friend or an adult to time you. How quickly can you put each word in the correct box? Practice putting information in the right place and you will find success!

CD Player	Concert	Potato	Beef	Tricycle
Train	Skates	Radio	Motorcycle	Peas
Sing	Peanut Butter	Airplane	Boat	Tuba
Banana	Sandwich	Ice Cream	Ketchup	Cookie
Walk	Piano	Truck	Drums	Car
Space Shuttle	Bus	Notes	Rock Star	Spinach
Milk	Bicycle	Dance	Baby Stroller	Apple

Transportation	**Music**	**Food**

Activity 17

Getting Ideas Out of Your Brain—It Only Takes Practice and Isn't a Pain!

Aldo was a kid who could do almost anything, at least his friends thought so. If kids in the neighborhood couldn't figure something out, they usually went right to Aldo's door. Sometimes grownups asked him for help too! Aldo knew how to fix bikes, paint a model, train a dog, make chocolate sauce, and help a baby stop crying. Plus, he could speak and write in both English and Spanish. But there was something that Aldo wasn't good at. He couldn't remember facts very well, and sometimes this was a problem.

One day, at school, he became really upset with himself. The class was studying state capitals and Aldo had done his best to study. But when he had to say them out loud in class, he froze!

"Uh . . . Columbus . . . yeah, that's Ohio . . . let's see, New York, no that's a state . . . OK . . . Orlando . . . no, that's a fun place to visit, not the capital of Florida . . . uh . . . for Texas, Houston . . . no it's Austin . . . no, maybe it's Houston . . . who knows?"

When Aldo got home, his grandfather could see that Aldo was not happy. Aldo told him what happened at school.

"Aldo," said his grandfather, "let's play a game that will train your mind to quickly find an answer." Aldo's grandfather continued, "I want you say the names of things that start with the letter T. Say anything that comes to mind. And Aldo, we will do it in English first!"

Aldo began to list things that began with the letter T. It was hard at first. But then Aldo thought to himself, "I am going to think of groups of things . . . like foods!" So Aldo said, "Tomato, tortilla, taco, toast, turkey, turnips, tea." All of a sudden, Aldo didn't have such a bad problem with memory. Instead of just thinking here and there, he thought about one group of ideas at a time. Next he thought about sports: tag, tetherball, tight end, touchdown, time out. He just got better and better!

After he had practiced with the letter T, he picked words that belonged to the group that started with other letters. Aldo looked over his lists once a day so that he could train his brain to remember what he knew.

You also can train your brain to remember what you know. Look at the chart below. Aldo wanted to keep up his memory skills. So he made a chart like this. With his grandfather's help, he listed all sorts of groups. He wanted to see how much information he could list in each group. See where Aldo wrote "states"? Under the word, he began to write all the states he could think of. He had his grandfather time him, just for fun. Take a look at what Aldo answered. Now, fill in the rest of the chart. Pick a group that is interesting to you. You might chose types of bugs or names of movies. See how well you can fill in your chart. And remember, practice works!

States		
Alabama		
Arizona		
California		
Delaware		
Florida		
Georgia		
Hawaii		
Idaho		
Kentucky		
Louisiana		
Mississippi		
Maine		
New Mexico		
Pennsylvania		
Rhode Island		
South Carolina		

Activity 18

Learn a Little Every Day . . . Help Your Brain Go All the Way!

Have you ever thought, "How am I going to learn all of this stuff?" If you are starting a new grade, or if you are studying for a test, that idea might pop into your head. In fact, it might stay in your head, making you a very worried kid.

Hey! Stop worrying! If starting a new school year feels like you are looking over a huge ocean that you have to cross, remember that no teacher will give you more than you can learn in a year. And even if it feels scary, if you learn how to use some simple tools, you can be a winner on even the hardest tests.

One important tool is to do a little every day. Students who enjoy school and who do well make sure that they learn something new every day, sometimes even on weekends! How does this plan work?

Just as your body needs exercise, your brain can't be a "couch potato." Think about how you would feel if you sat around the house for weeks and then decided to run a race. Chances are that you wouldn't be at your best. You would be slow and tired. In the same way, your brain needs daily "exercise." If you sit in school and shut off your thinking, or if you don't do your homework, your brain will be S . . . L . . . O . . . W. If you don't want a slow brain, keep it moving!

Kids who do well in school don't try to learn everything all at once. That would be impossible for anyone! Take a subject and break it down into small parts. Then make a written plan or chart that tells you (and maybe your parents) when you will learn certain things. When you learn them, mark it on the chart. If you have a hard day, write down what you will try the next day or write a note reminding yourself to ask for help. Your chart could look something like the one on the next page.

Sample Plan for Reading	Sun	Mon	Tue	Wed	Thur	Fri	Sat
Read pages 1–10 of chapter 1		I did a great job!					
Read pages 11–20 of chapter 1			√				
Study vocabulary words				hard words... get help			
Answer practice questions at end of chapter 1					√		
Review words and questions						review 3 times	
Relax!							√

My Plan for _____	Sun	Mon	Tue	Wed	Thur	Fri	Sat

Think about Dione. Dione loved to read, but she didn't like to spell. She thought that she could never learn to spell all of the words she needed to remember. In fact, one day, she looked at the dictionary in the school library and almost fainted! Then Dione's teacher, Mr. Sing, had an idea. He gave her a list of 100 spelling words. At first, Dione wanted to run out of the room!

Look at all these spelling words Oh my!

"Don't get upset," he said. "I promise you that you will know these words by the end of the year." Even though Dione wanted to leave the room, she trusted Mr. Sing and listened.

"I am going to help you learn one word a day. It will be just one word, but you are going to really study it."

Mr. Sing gave Dione a piece of paper with the word "cyclone" written on it. Dione didn't like that because "cyclone" was the kind of word that made her worry. The "y" and the two "c's" confused her. But Dione wrote the word again and again in her free time, and she repeated it before she went to bed. She had her grandmother test her on it. And guess what? She learned that word and never forgot it. By the end of the year, she had learned the "impossible" list of 100 words! You can do this too.

Just as Dione learned one word each day, you can make yourself learn one, two, or three interesting facts every day. This doesn't have to be all about schoolwork. You could learn a science fact from a television show or a book, or you could learn about the news from your parents or by reading the paper. You could discover stuff in your own backyard. If there are 365 days in a year, imagine what you will know on this date next year!

In the spaces below, list three new things you learned today. Remember, they don't have to be big ones!

1. _____

2. _____

3. _____

Activity 19

Do Your Best Every Day and Success Will be Your Pay!

Natalie and Erica were cousins. They were usually the best of friends, even though Erica was two years older than Natalie. Natalie had fun spending time with Erica, except for one problem. Erica was always two grades ahead of Natalie, and she would tell Natalie all that she was learning in school. This made Natalie very nervous and worried because she never thought she would be able to learn all that "hard stuff."

"How in the world will I ever pass that grade?" Natalie thought to herself. "Erica knows so much more than me! How will I ever learn all of that?"

One day Natalie told Erica how she felt. "Natalie," said Erica, "I don't want you to worry! Here are some ideas that help me do my best and show what I know in school."

- "The most important thing to remember is that you can't learn everything all at once," said Erica. "Even the smartest kid in the world couldn't do a whole year's work in a day! It takes everyone time to learn."

- "Every day that you are in school is important. If you keep telling yourself that it is OK to waste time, you will never do your best. You should keep an 'I can do it' attitude. You should not tell yourself, "Maybe I will try hard tomorrow if I feel like it." "

- "Learning is like building a house." (Natalie knew a little about building a house. Her family just moved from an apartment to a new house that was built just for them!) "Remember when they started building the first floor? Well, if the carpenters had been lazy and not measured correctly as they worked on the first floor, what would have happened when they tried to add on the second floor? It would have been a mess, all tilted and ready to fall down! When you learn, you also have to try hard from the start. Then everything you learn later will fall into place."

- "Think about all you have learned each day!" Don't worry about what you will have to learn the next day or in the next grade. At the end of every school day, write down a little note about what you have learned that day. This will make you feel a lot better." Erica then drew a chart to help Natalie keep track of all she learned every day. It looked like the chart on the next page.

Erica came over to Natalie's house the next week to help her fill in the chart. They started on a Monday. Natalie wrote that in Spelling she learned about words that had two "e's" (like "feet") or two "o's" (like "boot"). She felt pretty proud of that because she had always had trouble with those kind of words. In Science, Natalie wrote that she learned about why the sun rises and sets. The next day, she learned why the sun sets and rises at different times. Natalie also learned about Mathematics. On that Monday, she was able to remember the entire "9's" multiplication table. Whew, that was a lot! Now Natalie began to feel better. "See, I can learn every day. I'm not going to be afraid of failing. If Erica can do it, so can I!

Look at Natalie's chart.

Natalie's Sample Chart: What I Learned Today

Monday

Subject	What I Learned Today
Spelling	Words with two of the same letters next to each other
Science	Why the sun rises and sets
Mathematics	My entire nine times table!

Tuesday

Subject	What I Learned Today
Spelling	Words that end in "-ing"
Science	Why the sun rises and sets at different times
Mathematics	The 12 times table!

With a little help from your teacher or someone in your family (or even a great friend or neighbor!) make your own "What I Learned Today!" chart. Here is one for you to use. You might want to make your own if you need more room. You could even add some artwork to make it special. Keep doing this every day and you will see how much you can learn. And remember, always do your best every day!

What I Learned Today!

*Day*_____

Subject   **What I Learned Today**

_____   _____

_____   _____

_____   _____

*Day*_____

Subject   **What I Learned Today**

_____   _____

_____   _____

_____   _____

*Day*_____

Subject   **What I Learned Today**

_____   _____

_____   _____

_____   _____

*Day*_____

Subject   **What I Learned Today**

_____   _____

_____   _____

Activity 20

Don't Let Homework Ruin Your Day. Learn To Do It Your Own Way!

Unlike you, homework doesn't have a brain! That might sound funny, but it's true! Homework is just homework! You might think that your book bag growls at you, "Come here little kid . . . I am waiting to ruin your day!" But that is just your imagination talking.

Many kids will do anything to get out of homework, even though it helps them learn and do their best on tests. They never learn to take control. Instead of being the boss of their study time, they let the homework rule their lives! They never think of ways to be a "homework hero." Instead, things get worse and worse for them, and tests become a nightmare! Here are stories about what you shouldn't do!

- Edwin often doesn't tell his parents the truth. He knows that he has homework, but he makes up stories. "I did it on the bus!" or "Ms. Gerber never said we had to read that chapter." This is the worst thing a kid can do. It is always wrong to lie. It gets you in a lot of trouble. Your parents and teachers lose respect for you. And you lose respect for yourself.

- Coco just makes believe that the whole problem will go away. "I'm going to just forget about my homework and think about other things." That might work for a little while, but soon trouble will be coming! Coco might forget about her homework, but her teacher won't!

- Ian whines and complains over and over again about his homework. Sometimes his parents get so tired of it that they tell him to skip his homework. But the next day, it just comes back!

- Janet spends hours doing her homework, but she hardly gets anything done! She can't ever find the supplies that she needs. She jumps from one thing to another and never finishes anything. Soon Janet thinks that she isn't smart, even though she is a sharp kid!

- Tonya gets so upset that she sometimes waits until it is too late to do her homework. "It looks like a huge mountain to me!" Tonya thinks to herself. Since she thinks she can't climb that huge mountain, she never tries. She gets used to giving up.

- Jin races to get his work done. If you watched him, you would think there was a tornado in his room. Well, no one can do work that fast, but all Jin wants to do is finish. He might finish, but his good grades will be finished too!

Everyone wants to get their homework done so that they can have fun. But everyone also has to do homework, so it is smart to find a way to do it the best way! Here are some ideas to make you a super "homework hero"! Soon, you will also be a "test hero"!

- Remember why homework is helpful. Teachers do not give homework to be mean. They give you homework to help you remember what you have learned during the school day. The more you learn, the better you will feel about yourself and about school and the better you will do on tests. So think about homework as making you a great student, not an unhappy kid! One kid printed a banner that he taped to his desk. It read, "HOMEWORK FEEDS MY BRAIN!" This is how he remembered why he did his homework.

- There are two very important things to do every day before you leave your classroom! The first is to make sure you know all about your homework assignments. You don't want to do too little, too much, or the wrong thing! Some kids use a daily homework sheet to help them remember. It could look like this!

My Homework Log

Date _____

Subject	**Homework I Need to Do**	**Finished**
_____	_____	☐
_____	_____	☐
_____	_____	☐
_____	_____	☐
_____	_____	☐
_____	_____	☐

The second important thing to do is to check your book bag! It is easy to forget to take home stuff that you need to do your homework. Do you have all your books? How about your study sheets? And don't forget that list that tells you what you have to do for your science project! If you can count to 60, you can do this. It should only take you about 60 seconds (that's one minute) to do this important checking.

- When you get home, open your book bag and take everything out. That's right, EVERYTHING! Besides finding all that you need to do your homework, you might find some interesting things too, like a hundred-year-old apple or 26 cents in change!

- Next, lay out everything on a table. Look at your homework assignments and pick out what stuff you need to do your homework. Then put everything else back in the book bag.

- Then, get your brain ready to rule! You decide what to do next. Some kids do short assignments first. Other kids save those until last and do the hardest stuff first. Some kids like to read first, and some like to do math or write. Parents also know a lot about how you learn, so talk to them about it. Faith's parents knew that she could read forever. So they suggested that Faith do her reading last. This would give her something fun to do later. Faith also wanted to do her math before her noisy brother came home and bothered her. This was a good plan.

- Everyone needs a break! Some kids need a break every few minutes and some can wait longer. It is your job to figure out when you should take a break and what you can do so that the break helps you go back and learn some more. Many kids have a favorite afternoon TV show. When is yours? Ask if you can take a break and watch that show. But when the show is over, you have to go back and finish that homework! Starr begged her mother to let her watch "Powerful Princess" at 4:30 p.m. This didn't turn out to be a very good idea because then she wasn't in the mood to go back to her homework. Starr has to decide if she can really rule her homework.

- Find a time for an adult to check your work. Grownups are here to help you, even if it feels like they are a bother sometimes. Remember, you can be a bother too! So let them help you.

- Put all your work neatly back into your book bag. Ask yourself, "Where is my math homework? Is it in the notebook? Did I remember to take back my science book?" It is not very smart to do your work and then forget to bring it back to school!

Now it is time for some fun! Try to find all the stuff that a kid might find in his or her book bag! Some are pretty weird!

Banana	Pencil	Paper	Monster
Dinosaur	Book	Socks	Pen
Grades	Gloves	Candy	Tape
Marker	Keys	Glue	Mouse
Notes	Money	Lunch	Eyeglasses

```
E  C  G  H  B  F  F  R  I  B  C  G  H  D  S  C  S  R  V  M
Y  E  Q  O  P  E  R  Z  U  D  B  W  T  K  V  F  C  M  P  O
E  T  O  Y  H  C  P  A  D  A  I  P  C  C  L  F  Y  H  P  U
G  K  C  M  J  E  Y  A  F  T  S  O  I  S  G  R  P  Y  K  S
L  Y  F  R  N  O  B  Q  T  Z  S  O  J  S  Z  J  G  B  Y  E
A  K  C  E  C  J  L  L  V  Z  E  K  N  R  M  T  V  B  M  R
S  Q  T  T  H  X  L  N  V  K  Q  J  E  I  R  J  A  M  G  F
S  Z  G  S  B  P  E  B  H  R  X  A  K  E  D  L  N  R  J  E
E  N  F  N  Q  P  N  A  H  Y  P  N  H  P  E  N  C  I  L  E
S  R  B  O  D  N  X  N  Y  E  R  C  L  X  U  R  Z  I  W  G
Y  M  N  M  D  D  Y  A  K  G  A  V  U  Z  L  H  T  A  P  D
M  L  S  W  B  P  W  N  W  E  Z  F  N  X  G  I  F  X  C  D
R  S  Y  P  U  M  P  A  T  W  S  W  C  H  O  T  V  K  N  Z
S  E  D  J  S  H  G  P  S  Q  U  H  H  G  O  O  P  T  A  P
M  V  P  K  G  L  O  H  J  Q  Y  Y  R  P  B  C  R  S  Y  T
Q  A  C  A  O  S  E  D  A  R  G  E  S  Y  E  K  A  N  G  Q
N  E  R  V  P  V  T  E  K  R  R  N  I  M  Z  J  H  N  O  X
E  M  E  K  O  R  W  T  U  E  F  O  G  N  O  T  E  S  D  Z
W  S  P  B  E  V  O  A  O  K  W  M  Q  A  P  J  L  J  Q  Y
K  F  S  V  H  R  L  Q  J  B  I  T  F  I  G  U  X  B  W  Y
```

I can make the most of my study time! Here's how I am going to do it!

☐ I will keep my brain neat and tidy. I will put new facts in order.

☐ I will train my brain to remember what I know.

☐ I won't wait until the last minute to study. I will learn a little every day.

☐ I will do my best every day.

☐ I will keep a homework log. My log will let me know what my assignments are.

☐ I will keep my book bag neat and will make sure to bring home what I need to be a "homework hero."

☐ I will remember to bring my finished homework back to school.

Chapter 5

It's Almost Test Time

In this chapter, you are going to learn what you can do before the day of a test to help you prepare. When you know how to get ready for tests, you will be better prepared to do well on tests.

In This Chapter . . .

Activity 21

Get Your Rest Before the Test!

Miguel's big sister had a wonderful party planned. She was getting married soon and everyone in the family (and it was a LARGE family!) was coming over to tell her how happy they were for her. Miguel's sister asked Miguel to do something special at that party. Because he had a great singing voice, she wanted him to sing two songs for the guests. He was going to use a microphone, just like a rock star!

The day of the party, Miguel was a busy kid. First he went to the swimming pool with his friends. Then he rode his bike to the mall and looked at video games.

Miguel's father told him to rest, "Miguel, you are going to be too tired at the party!" But Miguel wouldn't listen. He just kept going and going. Finally, it was time for the party, and then the time came for Miguel to sing.

Guess what? Miguel was so tired that his brain didn't work. He forgot the words to one song and he couldn't remember the beat of the music for the other song. His cousins started laughing at him. Miguel couldn't show what he knew. He learned a very hard lesson. Next time he will make sure he gets enough rest.

It is important that you get enough sleep before a test. Sometimes this isn't very easy because kids are busy! They might have an activity the night before, or maybe they have a habit of staying up late, reading in bed. Lots of kids are really tired in the morning because they just don't get enough sleep.

Here are some ideas to help you get enough rest so that you can show what you know on tests!

- Try to go to sleep a little earlier each night of the week before a big test. Make a chart with your mom or dad's help. Write down the times that you will go to bed each day. If you do it without a frown, ask if you can have a treat at the end of the week! Your chart might look something like this.

My Plan for Going to Bed Earlier						
Sunday	**Monday**	**Tuesday**	**Wednesday**	**Thursday**	**Friday**	**Saturday**
3:00 p.m. tennis match	4:00 p.m. video games	5:30 p.m. dinner	6:30-7:30 study time	7:30-8 p.m. talk with mom about test	**Test Day!**	**TREAT!**
5:30 p.m. dinner	5:30 p.m. dinner	6:30-7:30 study time	7:30-8:15 read for fun	8:00 p.m. bedtime		
6:30-7:30 p.m. study time	6:30-7:30 p.m. study time	7:30-8:30 p.m. TV	8:15 p.m. bedtime			
7:30-8:30 p.m. TV	7:30-8:45 p.m. TV or read	8:30 p.m. bedtime				
8:30-9 p.m. read	8:45 p.m. bedtime					
9:00 p.m. bedtime						

- Get relaxed before you go to sleep. You might want to take a warm bath or get comfortable under a soft blanket. Think happy thoughts and take long, deep breaths. Keep the lights as low as possible. Tell your family to keep as quiet as they can!

- Don't study right before bedtime. Instead, try to get your homework done before dinner.

Activity 22

Can You Give Your Brain a Good Breakfast?

Your brain has a lot of work to do all day long! Even if you are sitting around doing nothing, your brain never, ever stops working.

Just like your body, your brain can't work very well if it is hungry. If you don't feed your brain the right way, you won't be able to do your best. This is really true when taking tests because that is when your brain works the hardest!

What does your brain like to eat? Well, brains eat the same stuff you do! So if you eat junk, then your brain will not have the right stuff to be as smart as it can be. If you eat right, your brain will be able to show what it knows. Your brain might even thank you!

On the morning that you take a test, get your brain ready for action by eating a great breakfast. Here is what you should do.

- Don't eat lots of sugar. Sugar stops you from being hungry for a while and it tastes good, but then it makes your brain tired!

- Eat some cheese, eggs, meat, beans, or milk. These foods are called proteins. They give you energy all day.

- Eat bread, tortillas, or rice. Those foods will also give your brain energy to do its best.

What would you eat for breakfast to help your brain be the best? Circle the best answers . . . you don't have to eat them all at once!

Pizza with Cheese

Scrambled Eggs Wrapped in a Tortilla

A Cupcake and a Glass of Sugary Fruit Punch

Fruit Rollups and a Soda Pop

Leftover Red Beans and Rice from Dinner
Last Night

Whole Wheat Toast with Peanut Butter

Chocolate Flavored Cereal
with Sugar and Milk

Sausage and a Biscuit

A Big Donut Filled with Jelly

A Big Glass of Milk and Two
Pieces of String Cheese

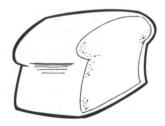

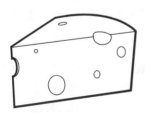

Activity 23

What Is Your "Game Plan"?

Having a "game plan" means than you plan what you will do before you face a challenge. No winning team in football starts a game without a game plan. The coach figures out what plays work the best and when to use those plays. He thinks about the skills of all his players and how to use those skills to win the game. Then, when the game begins, he can make sure that his players show that they can play great football!

A test is also a challenge, just like a football game. To show all that you know on tests, you need a game plan too. This game plan should help you figure out what you will do before and during a test. Here are some ideas that work, but every kid will want to make his or her own special plan!

- A few days before the test, look through this book again. Ask yourself if you need to practice any of these skills before the day of the test. Maybe you think that you still need a little help if you get stuck on an answer. Get a sticky note and mark that page. Find a teacher or a parent and ask that person to help you be cool with this test-taking tool!

- Think helpful thoughts! Do this while studying or at any time before the test. Tell yourself that you will do your best! "I am going to beat that test monster" or "I've done hard things before and I can do it again" are thoughts that make you stronger. If you want, go to a teacher or a parent and ask that person to cheer you on. It always helps to have people on your team saying, "Go, kid, go!"

- Get rest and eat right! Plan what time you will go to bed the night before the test so that you get enough sleep. If you have an evening activity the night before a test, ask your family if they think this will get in the way of a good night's sleep. If it might be a problem, think of an answer together. Maybe your parents could change your schedule, or maybe you would feel relaxed and sleepy if you took a warm bath before you went to bed. Watch out for that sugar at breakfast! The test monster would love to see you eat sugar at breakfast. "Ha ha ha . . . every mouthful of sugar makes it easier for me to win!"

- Think about how you will behave during the test. Plan to pay attention to yourself and the test and do not pay attention to other students. Looking at what others are doing doesn't help you at all. Remember to look at the teacher, to stay quiet, and to listen carefully to spoken directions. Practice this in your imagination. Don't forget that there will be lots of time to talk and play after the test!

- For fun, and to relax a little, create a doodle or symbol that shows how special you are. If a soccer team can be the "Roaring Lions" you, too, can be something super. Andy thought he was a quick thinker, just like a fast snake. So he drew a snake and called it "Smarty the Snake." Every time he looked at it, he knew that he would do fine on his test.

- Before taking a test, make a list of the most important test-taking tools that you must remember! Say them or write them a few times every day. Using these tools should be as easy as knowing your address . . . you don't even have to think about it! Roberto made a list like this. He also drew his doodle "Roberto the Ruling King." It was the face of a king with a crown.

MY TEST-TAKING GAME PLAN! GO, ROBERTO, GO!

1. I will fill in the answer bubbles with dark marks!

2. I will read the directions twice.

3. If I get "stuck," I will go on to the next question.

4. I won't talk to Rosalie during the test!

5. I will remember that I can do a lot of things, like play great soccer!

Just like Roberto, make your own "game plan" in the space below. You might want to make your own doodle, too!

MY TEST-TAKING GAME PLAN!

I know what to do around test time! Here's what I am going to do!

☐ I will get enough rest before the test.

☐ I will eat a good breakfast.

☐ I will have a game plan.

Chapter 6

Test-Taking Hints

In this chapter, you are going to learn what you can do during the test to help you do your best. When you know hints for test-taking success, you will be better prepared to do well on tests.

In This Chapter . . .

Activity 24

Pay Attention to What Is Most Important . . . the Test!

School is a busy place. That is part of what makes school fun and exciting for most kids. Many classrooms have lots of decorations on the walls, supplies and books on shelves, and a blackboard full of the teacher's writing. Some classrooms even have a pet turtle or a mouse! And every classroom has lots of activity, with kids working on computers, asking questions, and moving around. Part of growing up is learning to ignore all of these distractions when doing schoolwork. The better you pay attention, the more you learn. Then you can really show what you know!

During tests it is also important to pay attention. That is not very easy to do. Our eyes want to wander over to see what our friends are up to. We wonder, "How is my friend Marcus doing on the test? Is Brendan making a silly face?"

It is also easy to look around the room and forget about the test. You might find yourself thinking, "Did the mouse eat its food today? Why did Miki get a check mark by her name on the board?"

Remember that if your mind can't pay attention to the test, you might be the next one with the bad check mark!

The picture on the next page shows a classroom. In the classroom we see that Chad is taking a test. There are many things in this room that can get in the way of Chad paying attention. Circle at least three things that can get in the way of Chad doing his best on the test. Then, in the spaces below the picture, write a short sentence about what Chad was thinking when he let these things take his mind off what is the most important . . . his test! You can also draw in some great ideas of your own.

Chad

Miki ✓

Activity 25

If You Get Stuck, Don't Give Up!

Sooner or later, everyone has problems that they can't solve right away. They look at the problems and think about the problems and look at the problems some more, but their minds are blank. The answers just don't come, and people feel "stuck." Here are some things you should NOT do if you can't answer a question or solve a problem on a test.

Don't start thinking that you can't do anything right. Those ideas are wrong and will make you feel even worse. No one is supposed to know everything. Sometimes kids or adults can't remember an answer right away. Sometimes they should have studied a little harder. Sometimes worrying gets in the way of showing what they know. It is only a question. If you miss a question, it doesn't mean that you are a bad kid or a poor student. It doesn't mean that you will never do well in school. All it means is that you had trouble on one thing. The more you worry, the harder the test will be.

Don't give up! Skip that question and go on to another one. When you go on, many good things happen. One, you get less worried and stressed. Two, you have time left to do well on other questions. Three, as you take the rest of the test, you might suddenly remember what you forgot! You can then go back and answer the question that you skipped.

Don't let your body drive you crazy! When people feel stuck their hearts might begin to beat really hard. They might have trouble breathing or may feel dizzy. They might get stomachaches. If you start feeling that way, take a minute to close your eyes and take a few deep breaths. Tell yourself that you will do fine on the test. Remember, no matter how you do, your teacher still cares. Calm down your body and mind so you can go on to be a test hero!

Taking a test is a lot like going through a maze. You can't get upset when you hit a wall. You just have to go back and find another way. Try the maze on the next page. It's not easy, but you can do it. When you get stuck, don't worry. Use what you have learned to calm down and to find an answer. Now let's have some fun!

Start

You're Not
Stuck
Anymore!

Activity 26

Give Yourself a Rest, Don't Speed Through the Test!

Which of these ideas are NOT true about taking tests? (Make a check mark next to the correct answers.)

☐ The kids who do best on tests go the fastest.

☐ Your mind works better when you rush through a test.

☐ Most students never have enough time to finish a test.

☐ Checking your work is a waste of time.

☐ The smarter you are, the faster you do your work.

☐ Reading directions takes up too much time.

☐ If you don't finish every question, you will fail.

☐ It is better to quickly choose the first answer that comes to your mind.

☐ If you can't stand tests, you should get it over as quickly as you can.

Guess what? ALL of these ideas are WRONG! The truth is the opposite. Students who take their time on tests do better than students who race, rush, and speed.

Smart kids know that it takes time to figure out a problem. Sure, some kids do work faster than others, but the ones who do their best (remember that the most important thing is to do your best, not worry about what others can do) take their time to show what they know. These kids don't think about speed. Instead, they think about using their test time to find the best answers. They don't want to be slow pokes, but they also don't want to act like speeding bullets. They don't care if they are the first ones finished. They only care that they do a good job.

Some tests are harder than others, but tests are given so that you can show what you have learned. Most kids can finish tests, and if kids don't finish every question, it doesn't mean that they will fail.

Believe it or not, the best way to spend your time on tests is to read the directions and to check your work. It is easy to say, "I don't need to bother with directions," or "I don't have time to check my work." Reading directions and checking your work takes time, but it is worth it. Did you know that if you spend just five extra minutes going over directions and making sure your work is correct, you could improve by a whole letter grade? That's amazing, but it is true! Try it and see.

Lots of times it seems easier to try to hurry up and to get done with something you don't like. That is one reason why kids rush through tests. They think to themselves, "Please, let it be over!" That idea isn't very helpful. If you rush through something, you will never learn to do it better. If you slow down and try to figure out how to succeed, you will do better, not just on that test but on all your tests.

Give Yourself a Rest . . . It Works!

Don't Speed Through the Test!

Here is an exercise that will help you remember that rushing does not help you do your best.

Using a program on the computer, open a blank document. Put your fingers on the keyboard and find the vowel letters: a, e, i, o, u.

Have a friend or parent time you with a watch or a clock. Take your time and type these letters in order. Press "Enter" after each line. Type it as <u>carefully</u> as you can for 30 seconds. When Morgan tried this exercise, her paper looked like Step 1.

After you finish, count up how many lines had mistakes and subtract them from your total number of lines. That is the correct score. Use the chart on the next page to keep track of how well you did.

What is Morgan's correct score?

```
    9 Complete Lines
-   2 Mistakes
-----------------------
    7 Correct
```

aeiou
iaeou   (mistake)
aeiou
aeiou
aeiou
aeiou
aioou   (mistake)
aeiou
aeiou

Step 1: Morgan's Exercise

Now it's time for Step 2. Type again for 30 seconds. This time, you will rush through the exercise! Type as <u>quickly</u> as you can. Chances are that when you rush, you will have more lines but more mistakes. You will correctly complete more lines if you take your time and slow down. Record your results on the chart.

Although practice might help you a little, it is best not to rush. Instead, take your time and do your best!

Now it's your turn to try this exercise on a computer.

Step 1

Carefully type the vowel letters (a, e, i, o, u). After typing a line that contains each vowel once, press the Return or Enter key. Do this for 30 seconds.

Look at your letters. How many complete lines were you able to type? How many lines have mistakes? Fill in the information below.

_____ Complete Lines

— _____ Mistakes

_____ Number Correct

Step 2

As quickly as you can, type the vowel letters (a, e, i, o, u). After typing a line that contains each vowel once, press the Return or Enter key. Do this for 30 seconds.

Look at your letters. How many complete lines were you able to type? How many lines have mistakes? Fill in the information below.

_____ Complete Lines

— _____ Mistakes

_____ Number Correct

Which correct score is higher? Most likely, it's the score from Step 1 because you took your time. When you take your time, you pay attention to what you are doing and you do your best. Don't rush. It takes time to be your very best!

Activity 27

Following Directions Puts You on the Road to Success!

How can you do your best on tests if you don't know what to do? That might seem like a silly question, but think about it! You could be the smartest student in the whole world, but if you don't know what you are supposed to do, how can you show what you know?

Following directions can help you do a great job on tests. It takes some practice to be really good at following directions, but once you learn how, you will be amazed at how your test scores soar!

- Keep your ears open! Teachers will often tell you important information before the test begins. Be ready to hear what the teacher says by staying quiet. Keep your eyes on your teacher. If you talk to your friends and look around the room, those directions will go in one ear and out the other!

- Read all written directions twice! It doesn't take very long to do, but it will really stop you from making silly mistakes and from doing a lot of problems wrong.

- Talk to yourself when you read the directions. Ask yourself, "What exactly do the directions tell me?" If you read the directions, you should be able to give yourself answers to questions like, "What should I do first? What types of problems are these? Do I write a paragraph? Do I write a short answer? Do I show my work?"

- Make a circle or draw a line under important words in the directions. If the directions say "Write two sentences about pythons," you might want to circle the words "two" and "python." Then you will remind yourself to write more than one sentence and to be sure to write about those dangerous snakes!

- Paying attention and following directions carefully takes practice, but it is worth the time. You can become better at following directions in many ways. Listening to your basketball coach, helping your mom make brownies, or working on cars with your uncle are all chances to learn how to listen and do the right thing.

How well can you follow directions? Try this math trick! It won't work if you don't follow the directions!

1. Take your age or the age of anyone you know. (Ask your mom for her age, if she will tell you!)
2. Multiply that number by seven.
3. Take that answer and multiply it by 11.
4. Take that answer and multiply it by 13.

Your answer should have the age you choose first, followed a by zero, and then the age again. For example, if you choose the age of 12 and you follow the steps, your answer will be "12012." If you carefully follow the directions, it works for all ages.

Activity 28

Use Your Pencil to be a Great Test Taker!

Your pencil can be like a powerful magic wand when you take a test. Sure you need your pencil to write down answers and to fill in answer bubbles. But your pencil can do a whole lot more!

Use your pencil to help you pick the right answer. On multiple-choice questions, you can use your pencil to circle answers that you think might be correct. Then you can go back to them later and make up your mind. Or you can use your pencil to make a light line through answers that you think are wrong. Then you can try to figure out the right answer from the choices that are left. Desai used his pencil to help him answer the question below! Desai was asked which word should go in the blank.

> No one in the band was paying attention to what they were playing. Everyone was playing a different note at the same time. They should have been looking at the _____ to know what to do.
>
> **a.** boss
> **b.** conductor
> **c.** operator
> **d.** instruments

Desai thought about this question. He underlined important information in the question and then looked at the answers. He wasn't sure of the answer at first, but he did know that it wouldn't help if players looked at their instruments. That wouldn't tell them how to play. So Desai drew a light line through Choice D. Then Desai thought some more. He was pretty sure that he remembered that the person in front of the band is called the conductor. That was Choice B, so he circled that one. Later he came back to that question and looked at it one more time. He was sure that the word "operator" wasn't right, and he knew that no one "bossed" you when you played music. So he chose Choice B and was correct!

This is what Desai's paper looked like after he used his pencil.

Which word should go in the blank? <u>No one in the band was paying attention</u> to what they were playing. <u>Everyone was playing a different note at the same time</u>. They should have been looking at the _____ to know what to do.

a. boss

b. conductor

c. operator

d. instruments

Use your pencil to write down ideas that you will use later. On most tests, it's OK to write yourself little notes on the sides or the margins of the paper. You can use this space to help you remember or organize your thoughts. On mathematics problems, you can figure out answers to questions. Even if the test doesn't ask you to show your work, you can still use your pencil to help you find the right answer.

Spencer had to write a story about how to prepare for a trip on a sailboat. When he thought of ideas, he wrote them at the top of the page. Then he used these ideas in sentences later. Here is what his story looked like! Pay attention to what he wrote on the side of his paper!

How to Prepare for a Sailboat Trip

by Spencer T.

MY NOTES

safe shoes

no candy

camera

telescope

tell someone

If I was going for a long trip on a sailboat, I would first tell my mom what I wanted to do. I am still a kid and she has to know where I am. Then, if she lets me go, I have a lot of work to do. I would have to get enough food for a long time. It would be hot, so I don't want food that melts. Candy bars melt, so I can't bring any of them. I need new shoes too. You have to get shoes that don't slip or you can fall into the water. You need to bring games because it could be boring. It would be fun to bring a camera and a telescope. It is important to take pictures of your trip. It would be fun to look at stars. If you got lost, you could find the North Star and it would help you get home. I hope that doesn't happen.

Activity 29

Use All Your Knowledge . . . Act Like You've Been to College!

Sometimes kids forget how much they know! Although you learn a lot of important things in school, you have learned a lot in other ways. It might surprise you, but you probably know more than you think you do!

Using what you already know to solve problems is called using your common sense. You might have heard your parents or other adults talk about common sense. You might have heard them say, "Well, if you had used your common sense, you might have figured it out!" For example, Jesse's mother was upset because his older sister used almost a whole box of laundry detergent to wash her jeans. There were bubbles everywhere! When Jesse's mom got upset, his sister whined, "Well, how was I supposed to know what to do? I never did the laundry before! And anyway, the label was all wet and I couldn't read the directions!"

Jesse thought his older sister should have used some common sense. He thought to himself, "I've never done the wash, but I've watched my mom do it lots of times. I've never seen her pour a ton of detergent into the washing machine, even if she was washing my dirty soccer clothes." This was Jesse's first clue that you didn't need a lot of detergent to wash clothes.

Next Jesse thought about money. It didn't seem to make sense that it would take almost a whole box of detergent to clean one little pair of jeans. If that were true, no one would ever have enough money to clean their clothes! Jesse said to himself, "My common sense tells me that you don't need to use a bunch of soap."

Then Jesse looked at the size of the washing machine. "The inside of that machine is smaller than a bathtub. If I put a whole bottle of bubble bath in the tub, I'd have a bathroom full of bubbles and an upset mother too!" Even though Jesse didn't know exactly how to do the laundry, he knew what a mess too much soap could make. And laundry detergent is a type of soap.

Jesse might be younger than his sister, but he has more common sense. You can also use your common sense every day in your life and also on tests. In fact, using your common sense on tests will help make you a test hero!

Look at this test example to see how to use common sense to find a good answer!

> Shawna lives is a town called Sunny. The land in Sunny is dry, but the Sunny River runs through the middle of town. Drinking water for the town comes from the river, and farmers pump water from the river to help their crops grow. People also visit Sunny for vacations. They enjoy swimming and boating on the river. What will happen to the town of Sunny if there is a drought (very little rain) for more than three years?

If you were asked to write a short answer about this science problem, here are some common sense thoughts that might help you with your answer.

- I know that people use a lot of water for drinking and bathing. In my neighborhood, there are huge water storage tanks, so I have an idea of how much water a town needs. If the Sunny River was low, the town could run out of water.

- Most plants take a lot of water to grow. I know this because my mom has a garden. Once we were out of town and didn't water the flowers and tomatoes. They were all dried up in just a few days! Just think what would happen to the farmers' crops if there was not enough water! I bet that they will not grow, or at least they will not grow very much.

- If there isn't much water, people won't come to Sunny for fun. That could mean that people might not have jobs and everyone will have less money. I figured this out because lots of people work at the amusement park near my town, and if no one goes there, then there won't be anyone buying ice cream or going on rides. This means that there won't be jobs for the people who work at the park.

In the space below, write a sentence about a time that you used your common sense to figure out a problem.

_____

_____

_____

Activity 30

Fill in Those Bubbles or Your Life Will be Full of Troubles!

You have probably taken a bunch of tests in school. On some tests, you might have had to answer a math problem by writing the number answer. Sometimes you had to write the correct word, like on a spelling test. If the test was really hard, your teacher might have asked you to write sentences or paragraphs. On all of these tests (if you were neat!), the teacher could read your answers.

Some tests don't have written answers. Instead, students choose the right answer by filling in an answer bubble. Answer bubbles aren't very big. In fact, they are smaller than a jelly bean. But you have to fill in the whole bubble to show the right answer!

Most kids like coloring books. Filling in an answer bubble is a lot like coloring in the lines. A picture doesn't look very good with little tiny crayon marks. Just the same, an answer bubble should be filled in all the way! If you don't take the time to fill it in, trouble might be on the way!

Look at this example.

● **Correct**
✎ **Incorrect**

Practice Filling in the Answer Bubbles Here

Now, have some fun while practicing filling in bubbles! See all the bubbles, squares, stars, and triangles below? Only fill in the bubbles and you will find a secret message!

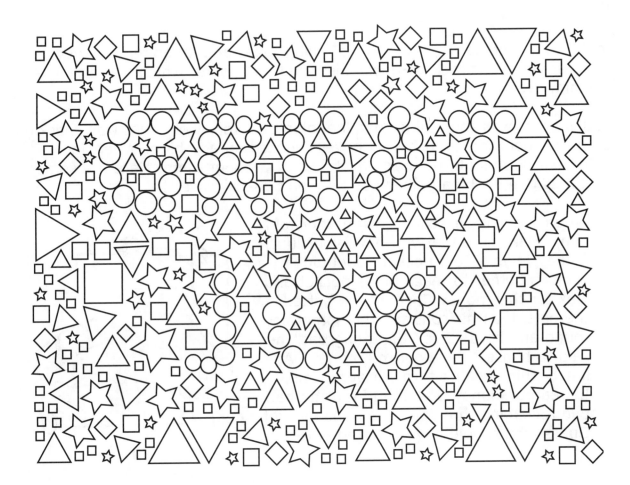

Activity 31

First You Look Once and Then You Look Twice . . . Checking Your Answers Is Very Nice!

Joel was a cool kid! He was always telling jokes and laughing. He even knew some magic tricks. He was also kind and polite, which made people like him even more.

Sadly, there was something that Joel didn't do very well. That was checking on his schoolwork. In fact, Joel never checked on anything! When Joel didn't check on stuff, he made mistakes . . . lots of them! Here are some mistakes that Joel made because he didn't check twice.

- When Joel left for school, his mother told him, "Make sure that you have your lunch money in your coat pocket!" Joel didn't want to bother to reach in his pocket and look for this money. Instead, he patted the outside of his coat and felt something round and hard. "Everything is great," he said to himself. "I've got my money." At lunch, things didn't turn out very well. Instead of money, Joel found that he had two rocks and three pennies in his pocket. Guess who should have checked twice!

- Once Joel was running late for school. He quickly reached into his sock drawer and pulled out two socks. For a second, he thought to himself, "I hope these are my blue socks," but he hardly looked at them when he put them on his feet and raced to the bus. When Joel arrived at school, all of his friends began to laugh and he hadn't even told one of his funny jokes! Why were they laughing? Because he had one brown sock and one black sock on his feet!

- Joel's older sister always helped him with his homework. The week before a big math test, they spent hours studying multiplication facts. Joel was sure he'd get an "A." He was so sure of himself that he never checked any of his test answers. That was not a good idea! He wrote "8 x 3 = 42"! He meant "24" but never looked twice. Then he answered "7 x 7 = 14"! He added instead of multiplying! Joel didn't get to show all that he knew!

Write about a time when you or someone you know didn't think twice. Remember that when you double check, you are checking to make sure you are correct. This is a good way to make sure you can show what you know.

_____

_____

_____

_____

_____

_____

_____

_____

_____

Activity 32

Ask Yourself, "What Do I Need to Know to Answer This Question?"

In the days when pirates roamed the seas and brave ship captains tried to safely deliver their goods, both the bad guys and the good guys had the same problem. They had to be able to see each other from long distances. The pirates wanted to find the next ship to rob, and the ship captains needed to know if pirates were nearby. To figure out this problem, young pirates or sailors climbed to the top of the sail to be lookouts. The lookout used a "spyglass" that helped him see things in the distance. Now you would think that being a lookout might be a dangerous job but also an easy one. There just doesn't seem to be much to see if you are in the middle of the ocean. But that's not really true! There was a lot to see, and to do a good job, the lookout had to pay attention to what was important and to ignore what wasn't important.

Of course, from way up high, you could probably see another ship, especially if you used a spyglass and the weather was clear. What other clues could be helpful? Sometimes looking at the ripple of the water gave clues. Ships would attract or sometimes scare away fish, and the movements of schools of fish might mean that a ship was close. At night, small sea creatures called plankton could be seen because plankton glow in the dark. It was sometimes possible to see the track of a ship by looking at the plankton. Using the sun was another trick. Sometimes, just for a minute, the sun would reflect off some metal on the ship, telling of its location. A flock of sea gulls was also a clue because it might mean that they were eating garbage from a ship. It was also important to ignore some of what could be seen. It would be easy to look at every bird and fish, even if they didn't give any useful clues. You could also look at the patterns in the clouds, which is fun, but not helpful. Most importantly, you had to pay attention because some clues weren't there for very long.

You will do your best on tests when you pay attention to what is important and ignore what you don't need to give the right answer. The best way to do this is to use a spyglass in your brain. Just like the lookout way up on top of the sail, ask yourself, "What do I need to find to answer this question?" Take a look at the math question on the next page.

Five families were crossing the country by wagon train. They picked Maggie Reinhard, a girl of 15, to keep a record of their journey. Part of the record looked like this.

	Pounds of Feed Used	**Miles Traveled**	**Type of Land**
Day 10	100	20	Rocky
Day 11	110	18	Rocky
Day 12	60	35	Grassy
Day 13	55	40	Grassy
Day 14	105	5	Woods
Day 15	110	8	Woods
Day 16	115	7	Woods
Day 17	50	31	Grassy
Day 18	20	2	Desert
Day 19	25	4	Desert
Day 20	65	29	Grassy

Now answer these questions by asking yourself, "What do I need to know?"

1. On what type of land did the families travel the farthest?

_____

Here the question asks you about the type of land and the miles traveled. You should only pay attention to that information.

2. How many miles did they travel altogether? _____

Here the question only asks you about miles traveled. Forget all the other information for a while!

3. How much feed per day do the animals eat on average when they are in

the woods? _____

Here the question asks you about how much the animals ate on days that they were in the woods. It doesn't ask you about rocky days, grassy days, or days in the desert.

4. On which day did they make the most progress? _____

This question asks about the best travel day. The answer doesn't look at the amount of feed or the type of land.

I know how to use test-taking hints! Here's what I am going to do!

☐ I will pay attention to the test.

☐ I will not give up if I get stuck on a question.

☐ I will take my time.

☐ I will follow directions.

☐ I will use my pencil.

☐ I will use all the knowledge I have learned in school and out of school to do my best.

☐ I will fill in the answer bubbles correctly.

☐ I will find out what the question wants to know and I will answer the question.

Chapter 7

Writing Strategies

In this chapter, you are going to learn about how to do your best when you have to write answers or responses on tests. When you know how to write well, you will be better prepared to do well on tests.

In This Chapter . . .

Activity 33

But I Don't Have Any Ideas! Use Your Imagination to be a Great Writer on Tests!

On some tests, you might be asked to write a story that you make up or to share what you think (this is called your opinion). Some kids think that this kind of writing is fun, but it drives other kids crazy! Those kids feel like they can't think of anything! If you are one of those kids, stop worrying. You can practice how to think of really super ideas and become a writing star.

Everyone has a bunch of important things to share. The problem is that all of these great ideas are locked in a "brain box" and you can't open the box without practice. The brain box is a silly way of talking about your memory. There is more information than you can believe in your memory. You just have to get to it! Just like training your dog to do a trick, you have to train your brain to open up these ideas.

You might not believe it, but you have had an interesting life. You have seen things, heard things, had feelings about things, smelled things, touched things, and tasted things. All of those experiences are somewhere in your brain box, which is a fun word for your memory.

Here's a Way to Use Your Imagination to be a Test Hero!

Allyson had to write a story about taking her dog for a walk. "I don't have anything to say," cried Allyson. "I just take my dog Frisky out and then we go home. I can't even write one paragraph about this!"

Allyson's mother saw that Allyson was upset. She put her arm around Allyson and said, "I have a way to help you make a great story! Let's draw a picture of you and Frisky going on a walk. In fact, let's make a quick drawing of you and Frisky getting ready for your walk, during the walk, and when you come home." Allyson's drawings weren't fancy. They looked like these.

  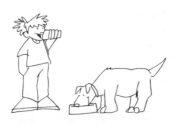

"Now let's talk about the first picture. What did you SEE in the house before you went on the walk? How did you FEEL? What did you HEAR?"

Allyson looked at the pictures and thought. She felt her brain box slowly opening. "Well, you were cooking dinner. And Frisky saw me and was running around looking for her leash."

"Great, you're doing fine," said her mom.

"And," said Allyson, "I was really happy to walk the dog and not do my homework!"

"Anything else?" asked her mom.

"Oh, I wanted to take Frisky next door and show her new haircut to our neighbor."

Before she knew it, Allyson had a lot to say about taking her dog for a walk. And she wasn't even halfway done with all the pictures or her memories. Allyson began to write, "When I went downstairs the other day, my mom was cooking dinner, but Frisky didn't care. All she wanted was to go for a walk. She ran around the kitchen because she knew that I was ready to get her leash. I was happy to take Frisky for a walk because I was tired of doing my homework. Plus, I wanted to show our neighbor her new haircut . . ." What a great start to a story!

In the box below, draw a simple picture of something that you did. Use it to open up your brain box (your memory). Then write a sentence or two about what you remembered.

Activity 34

Capitalization and Punctuation ... Don't Leave Them Out of Your Education!

Going to school and growing up can be very exciting. There is so much to learn, to do, and to think about. Sometimes parents complain, "Our kids go a mile a minute!" But parents are really happy when kids think life is great. Most kids have so much to think about. Whether it's friends, sports, movies, video games, or school, kids are always thinking about something!

Capitalization and punctuation help ideas make sense. If these helpful grammar rules didn't exist, all of our ideas would become one big and messy jumble! Think about talking. When we talk, we use capitalization and punctuation and we don't even know it. Our voices change just a little at the end of a sentence and at the start of a new one. When a sentence ends, just like a period, we take a tiny break in what we are saying. These signals help the people who are listening to understand what we are saying. When we keep talking and talking with no breaks, the listeners get mixed up or even upset! They probably will say, "We can't understand a word you are saying."

A fifth grader named David and his family lived on a farm. All year long he looked forward to the state fair. David would bring his pig Chester to the fair and would enter him in the prize pig contest, hoping to win. David spent a lot of time every day taking care of Chester and making him the best pig ever. He walked him for exercise, brushed his coat, fed him special food, and even cleaned his ears and teeth! The first two years at the fair, Chester didn't win. Finally, the third time Chester was in the contest, the pig came in second! Chester won a huge ribbon and David won $50!

The day that David and Chester won, David's grandparents came over for dinner. David could not stop speaking! Every word he said ran together like water in a river. He didn't even take a breath when telling his grandparents about the win in the pig contest. David's grandparents were very proud of his hard work, but they couldn't understand much of what he was saying! "David," said his grandmother, "you are babbling like a brook. You have to slow down. I can't tell where one idea stops and another begins." So David took a deep breath, finished his last bite of apple pie, and told his story with capitalization and punctuation. Now his grandparents know the whole story!

You will do your best on tests when you make sure to use capitalization and punctuation skills. It is easy to forget to do this in the middle of a test, but thinking about these skills and checking your work are very important! Ask yourself the questions at the top of the next page.

- Is there a period, a question mark, or an exclamation mark after each sentence? Is it the right mark for the sentence?
- Do I need to use any commas?
- Is there a capital letter at the beginning of each sentence?
- Did I capitalize important words, like people's names, the names of streets, cities, and states, things that have a title (like Eastwood Elementary School), or months and days?

If you can follow this simple plan, your test scores will soar!

Test Your Skills

This is a postcard from Ross to Simon. Ross went to the mountains on a camping trip and wanted Simon to know all about it. Sadly, Ross was so excited about his adventures that he didn't take the time to check his work. His spelling was fine, but his capitalization and punctuation were terrible! Can you find and fix his mistakes? Circle the mistake and then write in the correction.

---

august 15 2003

dear simon

hello from wild bear mountain? even though we didn't see a Bear we saw two elk and Six wolves I wasn't very scared but my friend jason was

on our way to the camp we stopped in denver which is a city in colorado oh and I forgot to tell you that we also saw mrs. miller right before we left she said good luck and gave us milky way bars for the trip

next time I hope that you can come with us

your friend

ross

There are at least 36 mistakes in this letter. If you can't find them all, ask a teacher or parent for help or look in the answer key at the end of this book.

Activity 35

Spell Carefully! What You Write May Not be Right!

Writing is an important way to share ideas. Without writing, it would not be possible for all that is known in this world to be shared with others. Think about a book that you have enjoyed reading. That author couldn't wait to tell his or her story. In fact, the author was so excited, he or she wanted to tell it to as many kids as possible. Well, if the author couldn't write it, how could the story be shared? Maybe the author could tell the story on television, but not many people get that chance. The author could go to many cities and towns, telling the story to groups of kids. But if you think about it, that's a little silly. If the author didn't write the story down and put it in a book, very few kids would ever enjoy the ideas. And the kids wouldn't have the book to read anytime they wanted, such as before going to sleep or in the car on a long trip.

Writing is an exciting skill that lets others know your special thoughts. If you write carefully, your ideas can be easily shared. But, if you aren't careful in what you write, it will be very hard to be understood.

A good writer does many things well. If you are writing a story or a book report, or are working on a project, you have the time and the chance to ask teachers and other adults for help. Many times, this helps you catch little mistakes. But when you take a test, you are on your own! If there are mistakes, it is your job to catch them. It's like fishing, only the fish are mistakes.

A big mistake that students make on tests is sloppy spelling! The good news is that by fishing for mistakes carefully, you can fix a lot of spelling errors. No one expects perfect spelling on a test (except on a spelling test), but if you know how to spell a word and don't use that word correctly, you are sure not showing what you know. Spelling mistakes happen for these reasons.

- Some words sound the same! Jose wrote "I left my baseball right <u>hear</u>." What he meant to write was "I left my baseball right <u>here</u>." Jose can win at baseball, but he's not winning at careful spelling!

- Some words look almost the same! Mae Ling wanted to describe her trip to the beach. She wrote "We made castles in the <u>send</u>." That didn't make any sense at all. She should have written "We made castles in the <u>sand</u>." She didn't catch her mistake because she didn't take time to fish for mistakes. Maybe she should have practiced fishing when she was at the beach!

- Many times, the way a word sounds is not exactly how it is spelled! Jamal answered a question about his pets. He wrote, "I am <u>unhapee</u> if I can't play with my dog every day." Jamal should have thought to himself, "This doesn't look right. There aren't many words with two e's on the end. I better check this word." Jamal was <u>unhappy</u> when he lost points for spelling!

A Secret Message for Good Spellers

Can you find the misspelled words in the paragraph below? Circle the words that are spelled incorrectly. Then take the first letter from each word that you circled and put it in the spaces below the paragraph. You will make a secret message!

Claudia and Amy are supor friends. They like to pley with their pets, make up games, and they enjoye lissening to music. Sometimes their moms will beg, "Leeve our ears alone and turn that noise down!" Most of the time Claudia and Amy will listen but once in a while they ignor what they are told! Nowe, they might as well forget giong to the mall or having a sleep over party! They complained, "We can't be good every hourr," evin though they knew what was rite. Claudia and Amy loved being best friends. "I wish we could be sisters!" they would think. "But, even though we can't be sisters, it is great that we will always have each othur."

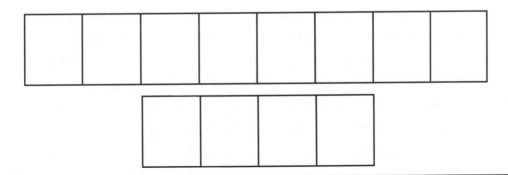

Activity 36

Your Bad Handwriting Can be Frightening!

Not every kid has the neatest handwriting, but almost every student can improve his or her handwriting. On most tests it doesn't matter if you print or use cursive writing. What matters most is that people can read what you wrote. If they can't, then how can you show what you know? And what about mathematics? Math isn't only knowing about numbers. You have to write them, too! If your writing is messy, you might get the wrong answer. And even if you figure out the answer, no one can read it! Remember, it is even harder to be neat on tests than on schoolwork. This could be a big problem. Don't get beat, get neat!

Here Are Some Ideas for Better Handwriting!

- How does your hand feel when you hold a pen or pencil? When writing, many kids' hands hurt and get tired when writing (this is true for grownups too!). This can happen if you hold the pen or the pencil the wrong way. Ask your teacher or parent for help. They may get a small holder that you put on your pen or pencil. The holder will make writing feel better.

- Copy the paragraph below on a lined sheet of paper. This paragraph includes every letter in the alphabet. It also has some letters that often go together. Show it to a few grownups, like your teacher or people in your family. Tell them to show you what letters or words are hard to read. Then practice writing those words and letters.

The bees in Mr. Jasper's fields were making quite a racket! They sounded like a million fighter airplanes all taking off at the same time. "Can anyone tell me what is going on?" cried Mr. Jasper excitedly. Soon, all the neighbors rushed over to his house. "We want to help you with the bee problem, but we don't even know how to start!" Suddenly, Mr. Davis, another farmer, raised his hand. Everyone was surprised because he was the laziest man in the county. He spoke, "Now I know that none of us are going to go into the fields and fix the problem. But remember that old hot air balloon in my barn? I'll get her up in the air and see what the problem is. And guess what? I'll do it alone, for free! It won't cost anyone a penny." Sure enough, Mr. Davis got that old balloon up in the air. Not very high, but it worked. And guess what he took up in that old thing? A horn! As he flew over the fields, he blew that horn. The bees went flying away! Then he landed his balloon and took all the honeycombs that the bees had made. Laughing to himself he said, "I have made a honey of a deal for a lazy man!"

Here are Some Ideas for Working with Numbers!

- You may have to write numbers when you answer a question. Practice lining up numbers in rows and columns by making addition and subtraction problems and solving them. Start with two number problems, then use three numbers. Check and check again whether you can read the numbers that you carry over from one column to the next. Then try some multiplication using two numbers and then three or more!

Michael made a practice sheet to help him learn to be neater in math. Can you find his mistakes?

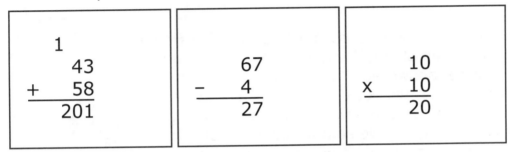

- Make sure that you can read the numbers that you write. Make sure others can read them, too! Look at some of your math homework. Show it to a few adults. Are any of the numbers hard to read? Write out the numbers 1 to 50 in the spaces below. How neat is your number writing?

Activity 37

Write to the Prompt to be a Powerful Writer!

DeShawn loved his Grandpa Hodge. Grandpa Hodge would take DeShawn fishing nearly every Saturday. Afterwards, they would go out for hamburgers and would talk for hours. But one thing bothered DeShawn about his grandfather. Sometimes, if he asked his grandfather a question, his grandfather wouldn't really answer him. Instead, his grandfather would tell a long story about something that didn't give DeShawn the answer he needed.

For example, one day DeShawn asked Grandpa Hodge, "What kind of bait should I use if the water is muddy?" His grandfather answered, "When I was a boy, the water was clear as glass. We could use any bait we wanted because the fish could see it all. And we used to get 50 cents for every fish we sold in town." DeShawn thought that was an interesting story, but he still didn't know what bait to use!

All of us have great stories to share, but on a test, we need to answer the question that is asked. The questions asked on writing tests are sometimes called prompts. To do your best on writing tests, you need to write about the question or the prompt that you are asked. And you have to stay on that subject! Here are some ideas to help you make sure that you don't answer like Grandpa Hodge.

- **Read the question or the prompt carefully.** In fact, read it twice! Look at this prompt: "If you could build a house any way you wanted, what would it be like?" For a good answer, you could write about the number of rooms, the color of the paint, whether there would be a swimming pool or a movie room, or if it would be in the city or in the country. It is easy to forget the prompt. You could start writing about what you don't like about your own house or apartment, or you could write about what you have to know to be a builder. These are interesting ideas, but they don't answer the prompt about your dream house!

- **When you have finished writing the first two or three sentences of your answer, read the question or the prompt again.** Then read what you have written so far. Are you answering the question that was asked? If not, back up and start again.

- **Write down ideas that will help you answer the question or the prompt.** You might want to write down memory words in the margins of your paper to help you remember good ideas that answer the question or the prompt. To help you write about your dream house, you might want to write "U.S.A., Red, White, and Blue" (to describe the paint) and "big bathtub in every bathroom." Then you can put these ideas in sentences.

- **Read your finished answer and make sure that you stayed on target!**

Here are some prompts to read. After each prompt, write some words or ideas that address the prompt.

> **Example:** "Why do you think that Ohio is special?"

> **You might want to write:** "great snow"
> "two football teams"
> "a lot of lakes"

Later if you want, you can write sentences about each idea to make a paragraph.

1. "Describe how you and your friends could prepare for Parents' Day at your school."

_____

2. "Do you think large or small families are better and why?"

_____

3. "Pick three jobs and give your opinions about why they are important."

_____

4. "What is your favorite day of the week and why do you like it best?"

_____

5. "What would it be like to be an astronaut?"

_____

Activity 38

Writing Powerful Paragraphs

A paragraph is a group of sentences that all work together to get a job done! Think about getting your friends together to plan a party to watch a big hockey game. There is a lot of work to do. Everyone has to figure out what food to bring. Your basement has to be decorated to celebrate this big event. Some of your friends will want to bring some games or videos for fun after the hockey game. But all of you have one goal! You want the best hockey party ever! All of you have to work together.

Now think about what would happen if some of your friends ignored the plans. Maybe one of them brought over baseball posters instead of hockey decorations. Maybe another brought over a boring cheese pizza, even though everyone had agreed that they wanted pepperoni! Now the party isn't holding together. It is still a party, but it could have been much better.

Sentences in paragraphs also have to work together. Just like planning a great hockey party was the main idea, paragraphs also have to have main ideas. All the sentences in a paragraph support the main idea, just like your friends supported each other when they worked together. When a paragraph has sentences that don't go along with the other sentences, it might still be a paragraph, but it could be a lot better. Remember, just like your group of friends, sentences that work together make powerful paragraphs! And they lead to better grades on tests!

Now, try out this idea on the paragraphs on the next page. You will see that each sentence in the paragraph is numbered. After you read the paragraph, circle the number of the sentence that does not belong. Remember, if you think about the main idea of the paragraph, it will be easier to figure out the answer. Then, write the main idea of the paragraph using your own words or copying from the paragraph.

(1) The Amish use old-fashioned skills every day of their lives. (2) They build their own barns, make butter in a churn, and sew most of their clothes. (3) My uncle used to make his own fishing rods. (4) The Amish still buy some things in stores that they can't make themselves, but they get to the store in a horse-drawn buggy.

A. MAIN IDEA: _____

(1) A museum is a place where you can learn about many subjects. (2) There are art museums that have paintings and science museums where you can try out different experiments. (3) There is even one museum that has a collection of dolls from all over the world. (4) You have to be careful not to touch or break the dolls. (5) Even if you have to travel a long way to get to a museum, it is worth the trip.

B. MAIN IDEA: _____

(1) Hosting our family reunion was fun. (2) I get sick of my cousins sometimes. (3) My mom and dad had more than 200 relatives come to our farm to meet. (4) Some of my aunts and uncles had not seen each other since they were my age! (5) At the end of the day, we had a picture taken of all of us together. (6) I learned that it is important for families to never forget each other.

C. MAIN IDEA: _____

(1) A lot of people think that taking a plane ride is easy, but that isn't always true. (2) Last summer I went with my stepmom to visit my brother and we went on an airplane. (3) First the plane was late. (4) Then a baby on the plane wouldn't stop crying, and you can't escape from that! (5) Believe it or not, the airline lost my suitcase and I had to wear the same clothes for two days. (6) Going on a airplane could help you decide if you want to be a pilot when you grow up.

D. MAIN IDEA: _____

Activity 39

Your Best Work Has a Beginning, a Middle, and an End

Marena has three brothers and one sister and all of them love movies! Marena's mom lets the kids pick one movie each week to rent and enjoy. That sounds like fun, but there is usually a problem. The kids are so busy that they can't all watch the movie at the same time. And that causes big mix-ups in movie watching!

Here is what happened one week. Marena and her youngest brother, Stefano, started watching the beginning of the "The Battle for the Magic Jewel," but then it was time to help with chores. So they stopped the movie. Ten minutes later Marena's oldest sister, Aquina, turned on the VCR and began watching the movie. But it didn't make too much sense to her because she had missed the beginning.

Then Julio and Edwardo came in and fast-forwarded the movie almost to the end. "We have to see the end because we are playing baseball all weekend and we won't have time to see the whole movie!" The boys thought that the battle scene at the end was cool, but they had no idea of what the whole movie was about because they never saw it! After they were done, they rewound the VCR tape backward and stopped somewhere in the middle. They were trying to be polite, but they had no idea where Marena, Stefano, or Aquina had stopped watching.

When Marena and Stefano finished their chores and turned on the movie, they were in the middle, but they hadn't even finished the beginning. Now it was their turn to be confused! Soon it was time to return the movie. It's not a surprise that when Marena's mother asked questions about the movie, no one in the family could give her an answer that made sense!

You might have great ideas, opinions, and stories to tell (you might even create wonderful movies someday!), but if you forget to use a BEGINNING, a MIDDLE, and an END, no one will understand what you are trying to say. When you are asked to write a story or to share an idea or an opinion on a test, you will show what you know if your writing is organized. Look at the three pictures below. Put these in the right order so that they tell a story with a beginning, a middle, and an end.

Here are some groups of sentences. In each group, there is a sentence missing. Create a sentence or two that makes a beginning, a middle, or an end so that the paragraph makes sense.

1. It is important to remember to check your book bag before you leave for

home. _____

_____. Now I have to do two nights of homework all in one day!

2. Sara wanted to make a special birthday gift for her grandmother. First

she went to the craft store to buy supplies. Then she spent hours

making a box that was covered in paper flowers and ribbons.

_____

_____

_____. Then her grandmother opened the box and found an even

more beautiful gift inside!

3. _____

_____.

"Where is your ticket?" asked the train conductor. "I better rush home and find it!" exclaimed the boy. "Stay on the train for now, son," replied the conductor. "We will worry about it when we get to New York."

4. Tucker lived with his parents on a farm. His dream was to grow the biggest and best pumpkin in the county. All summer long he watered his pumpkin patch. He covered the pumpkins with a blanket in the heat of the day, and he made sure there wasn't a weed within a hundred feet. All of his pumpkins were big and orange, but one was gigantic! It grew and grew until Tucker couldn't move it anymore. It glowed like an orange sunset! On the day of the contest, Tucker and his uncle used a crane to lift the pumpkin onto a truck and drove it into town.

_____

_____.

5. Now try to fill in two different parts of this paragraph.

_____

_____

_____. "This water really froze nice and hard on my homemade skating rink," thought Jamie. _____

_____

_____.

Thinking About the Main Idea Is a Great Idea!

Sierra was a smart girl. She usually made good grades in school and was great at playing the flute. But Sierra had a problem. Even though she had many good ideas about a lot of things, she didn't share them well with others. Sierra would get so excited that her words would come out like a big jigsaw puzzle that had dropped all over the floor! There would be one piece there and another piece over there, but no one could see the whole picture!

One day Sierra was trying to tell her stepdad that she didn't think her little brother was doing enough chores around the house. She had a really good idea to help her brother become more responsible, but she didn't just say, "Hey, I think if we put stickers on a chart, Jonathan might pick up his towels and clothes." She didn't get to the main idea, even though it was a great idea. Instead, she kept talking about her chores, and the kind of chores kids should do, and other things. Her stepdad was confused. If he had heard her wonderful main idea, he probably would have given Sierra a sticker!

If you want your ideas to be understood when you write, you have to show the main idea. This is especially important on tests. Students who are great writers know how to show the most important idea at the beginning of the paragraph.

Sometimes kids get mixed up when they have to think of the most important idea in a paragraph. Because they have many interesting things to write, everything seems like the main idea! Liam figured out a way to find the main idea. He tells himself, "If I was running away from 10 huge monsters, a swarm of 50 snakes, and a nest of scorpions, I would only have a minute to scream out my main idea! That would be, 'Send for help!' I would explain all the rest later!"

Look at the paragraphs on the next page. The sentence that gives the main idea is missing. The correct main idea sentence is one of the answer choices below the paragraph. Circle the letter of the correct answer.

1. _____. On the
Fourth of July, people share their pride in our country in many different
ways. Some gather in groups in thanks for our country. Many families
have picnics and are thankful for their freedom. They enjoy their time
together. Most people see fireworks. Flags fly all over the city in
celebration!

    a.   The Fourth of July is a great time to eat new foods.

    b.   Some people like to call the Fourth of July "Independence Day."

    c.   The Fourth of July is a celebration for all Americans.

    d.   Because the Fourth of July is in the summer, it is the best holiday.

2. _____. Twins
sometimes have to learn to do many things on their own because their
parents are so busy! They also have to learn to get along and share
because a twin is usually nearby. But the good news is that twins are
never lonely. Each twin has a playmate all the time. In fact, some twins
have their own "secret words" that no one else can share!

    a.   It is better not to have brothers or sisters.

    b.   Life is different when you are a twin.

    c.   Parents who have twins are often tired.

    d.   If you are twin, you probably won't be very happy.

3. _____. Some
people feel that no animals should ever be kept in zoos. They believe
that it is cruel to put animals in cages or pens. Others believe that zoos
teach people to understand and care about animals. They believe that
this protects animals that live in the wild because people will respect
them. Some scientists study zoo animals. They want to use this
knowledge to help all animals be healthy and survive.

    a.   People have many feelings about keeping animals in zoos.

    b.   Zoo animals have a hard life.

    c.   It is bad to argue about animals.

    d.   Taking care of animals is what everyone wants.

Activity 41

Spiders Can be Your Friends

Because he was the oldest kid in the family, Ethan thought that he knew everything. Well, he didn't really believe that he knew as much as his parents, although he acted that way sometimes! Ethan told his younger brothers what to do all of the time. Sometimes they listened, and other times they complained to their parents. But most of the time, they didn't let it bother them. Ethan also liked to tease others. The person he teased most was his sister Elana. He teased her because she always got so upset! Elana was scared of a lot of things, like thunder and high places, but she was especially scared of bugs. It would probably take a million dollars to get Elana to even go near a bug, and Ethan took advantage of that. "There's a bug in your hair!" Ethan would tell Elana. Elana would jump up and start running. Of course, Ethan would laugh.

One day Elana came home from school, "I got an 'A' on my report about France!" she told her mother. Ethan heard and he was jealous.

"How did YOU get such a good grade, little sister?" said Ethan rudely.

"Easily," smiled Elana. "A spider helped me."

Ethan couldn't believe his ears! His sister was terrified of any bug, particularly an ugly and hairy one. And anyway, he knew that bugs didn't go to school. "Yeah, that's a dumb story," he said.

"No, it's not," said his mother sternly. "Your sister has made spiders work for her, to help her show what she knows. Let's sit down and have her show us her spider trick."

Elana brought out a drawing of a spider. It was big, almost as big as the piece of paper. Her drawing had a body, six legs, and each leg had four hairs on it. It also had antennae. Words were drawn on all over the spider. It looked like the spider at the top of the next page.

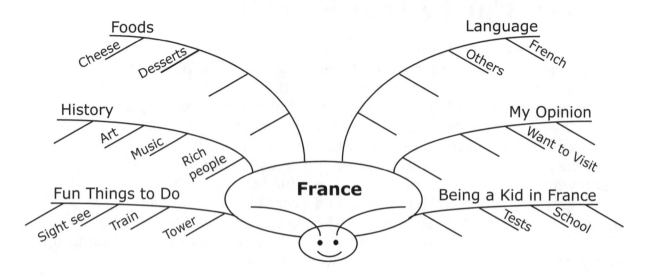

"Tell us how this helped," said their mom.

"Well, I put the main idea in the body of the spider. I had to write all about France. Then I got on the computer and went to the library. I started thinking about some ideas that would make good paragraphs, like what is interesting to see in France and what it would be like to grow up there. I wrote these ideas on the legs of the spider. Then, whenever I found some details, I wrote them on the hairs. Each leg would be a new paragraph!" This was Elana's report:

THE COUNTRY OF FRANCE

France is a country with a long and exciting history. France has given the world wonderful art and music, which we enjoy today. France is a nice place to live, but it wasn't always that way, unless you were the king or you were very rich. All the royalty and rich people lived in a huge palace called Versailles. It sounds like "ver sigh." Finally, all the poor people got sick of being treated badly and took over, but the palace is still there.

People in France make all kinds of cheeses, and some of the cheeses age in caves. France also has super desserts.

French is the official language of France, but a lot of people speak English and other languages too. French people like to speak French the best and wish that other people spoke it too.

Being a kid in France is a lot like being a kid in America. They have the same grades, but many kids learn English right from the start. They have tests that decide what high school or college you can go to. Kids usually have more homework too.

If you want to have fun in France, you can visit the palace or go to the top of the Eiffel Tower, which is a beautiful tower in Paris. You could travel around France on the bullet train, which is the fastest train in the world.

I think that France would be a great place to visit, but I still like my own country the best. I hope that the United States and France stay friends because we have a lot to share.

Guess who was "bugged" now? Ethan had to admit that his sister had some good ideas. And the next week, he used them to get an "A" himself!

You can use a spider to help you write, or you can create another picture that will do the same thing. Kids do lots of different things to help them tell a story or write a report.

Lyle drew a tree with many branches. Kenisha drew a wide river with smaller streams that ran into it. Jacinta drew a picture of the universe with a big star in the middle and larger and smaller stars around it.

Here is a spider for you to complete. You don't even have to go to the library or use the computer. Your job is to get ready to write a report about your school. Fill in the rest of the spider. Use each leg for different paragraph ideas and the hairs for details.

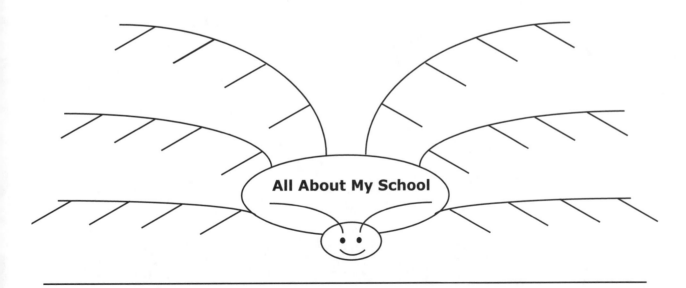

I can use writing strategies! Here's what I am going to do!

☐ I will use my imagination.

☐ I will use correct capitalization and punctuation.

☐ I will spell words correctly.

☐ I will use my best handwriting.

☐ I will write to the prompt.

☐ My writing will include a beginning, a middle, and an end.

☐ I will include a main idea.

☐ I will use a spider to help organize my thoughts.

Chapter 8

Reading Strategies

In this chapter, you are going to learn about how to do your best on reading tests. When you know reading strategies, you will be better prepared to do well on tests.

In This Chapter . . .

Activity 42

Know the Difference Between Facts and Opinions

Jared and Richard were having a friendly argument about basketball. "Magic Johnson is the best basketball player ever," said Jared. "He won an Olympic gold medal for the United States. He played every position in a championship NBA game and was on a team that won five national championships. He was voted the most valuable player (MVP) three times and was an All Star 12 times. He helps out kids and builds stores to give people jobs. He has a kind heart and is a nice person."

"Well," replied Richard, "Michael Jordan is the best! He won six championships and was an All Star 13 times. Besides that, he scored more than 30,000 points in his career. He scored more than 50 points a game in 36 games! Michael Jordan also plays golf and was a baseball player for a while. Because he is an all-around athlete, he does a better job at showing kids that sports are good for them. He's a lot better than your guy!"

When Jared and Richard talk about their favorite basketball players, they talk about facts and opinions. Facts are different than opinions and opinions are different than facts! A **fact** is something that can be proven true. An example of a fact would be, "Mexico is south of the United States." We know this is true by looking on a map. An **opinion** is how someone feels or thinks about something. An opinion might be, "Mexican tacos taste better than hamburgers." Some people might feel this way, but it is an opinion.

Both Jared and Richard shared many facts about Magic Johnson and Michael Jordan. But they also gave their opinions. Jared thought that Magic Johnson was kind. Richard thought that Michael Jordan was a better athlete. Both boys formed their opinions by learning about their favorite players and both used facts when giving their opinions. This helped their opinions make sense, but their ideas were still opinions, not facts.

When you are asked to read a passage and answer questions, it is important to think about facts and opinions. This will help you do your best on tests. Ask yourself, "Is the passage telling me facts, opinions, or both?" Then ask yourself, "Does the question ask me to write about facts or about my opinion?" It is important to make sure your opinions come from facts. But remember, an opinion is still what you believe or feel, it is not a fact.

Read the following sentences and write "O" on the line if it is an opinion, and "F" if the sentence is a fact.

1 **A)** If we paint the classroom blue, it will help everyone feel cheerful. _____

    B) This blue paint is the same color as the rug. _____

2 **A)** The temperature this morning is 85 degrees. _____

    B) It is too hot to have fun at recess. _____

3 **A)** Mustard doesn't taste as good as ketchup. _____

    B) Ketchup has more sugar in it than mustard has. _____

4 **A)** My dog barks every time I put on my Scout uniform. _____

    B) My dog would like to join our troop. _____

5 **A)** Shoveling snow is too much work. _____

    B) It takes about an hour to clear our driveway of snow. _____

6 **A)** My grandfather is the oldest person in our family. _____

    B) It isn't very easy being old. _____

7 **A)** At our school, the kids elect a student of the week, but at my cousin's school, the principal chooses the student of the week. _____

    B) It is more fair for students to choose who they think deserves to be student of the week. _____

8 **A)** My mom does not like to drive my dad's truck. _____

    B) Girls should buy cars, and they should not buy trucks. _____

9 **A)** Our zoo spent $10,000 to buy some peacocks from another country. _____

    B) It is a better idea to spend money on taking care of animals that are already in our zoo. _____

10 A) At the beginning of the school year, everyone must buy 10 pencils, five pens, three large erasers, crayons, and at least 500 sheets of notebook paper. _____

    B) It would be nice if students bought colored markers and tape at the beginning of the school year. _____

Activity 43

Read It All and the Test Monster Won't Call!

You might not believe it, but the test monster is always waiting to make sure that we don't do our best on tests. One of his tricks is to tell kids, "You don't need to read everything in a question! You will run out of time and you will not show what you know for sure! So hurry up and get it over with!" Then the test monster laughs to himself (not a very nice laugh as he has smelly breath and slimy teeth) because he thinks he fooled you into rushing and not reading everything on the test.

Luckily, you know more about tests than the test monster thinks you do. You would never skip over what you are asked to read! Instead you would tell yourself, "I have lots of time to read the questions and the answers. I probably have enough time to read them twice! And I can read them carefully, too!" The test monster isn't laughing anymore. In fact, he is crying (and that's not a nice sight either because his tears are as yucky as the rest of him). "Kids are getting too smart these days and I will be out of a job," the test monster cries. Too bad for that test monster!

Practice Reading It All

Look at the sentences below. The words are spelled correctly, but the sentences do not make sense. After reading the sentences carefully, write a few words about what was wrong with the sentence.

Example: I can't wait to get out my sled and ice skates when it starts snowing next summer.

Answer: It doesn't snow in the summer.

1. Aunt Karen has a big pond behind his house.

_____

2. The United States has sent astronauts to the moon and the sun.

_____

3. If you plan to bake a cherry pie, make sure to turn off the refrigerator after you are done.

_____

4. Our family didn't go on vacation until July although we planned to go the month before in August.

_____

5. My brother C.J., who just had his 8th birthday, will soon be going to college.

_____

6. There are 50 countries represented on the American flag.

_____

7. My dad's car got stuck because he didn't have any water in the tire.

_____

8. Make sure you erase what you typed on the computer so you can print it out later.

_____

9. When my dad and stepmom met with my teacher, I knew I was in trouble because there were four adults against one little kid!

_____

10. I better remember to use my thermometer to measure the distance between my bed and my dresser.

_____

Activity 44

Use Context Clues to Help You Become a Test Wizard!

"All this reading is driving me crazy," cried Reid. "It's just words, words, and more new words! Half of the time, I have no idea what they mean! I can't look every word up in the dictionary because I'll be 90 years old before I'm done!" Reid was so upset that he didn't even eat the cupcakes that his mother set out for his after-school snack. This was a bad sign because Reid was a cupcake fanatic. He could eat six chocolate cupcakes if his mom let him. For Reid, cupcakes were probably his all time favorite food.

Look at the paragraph above. See the word "fanatic"? This is a new word for many kids (and even some grownups). How can you figure out what it means? For many words, using context clues can help. Using a context clue means reading the sentence (or sometimes the paragraph) and using that information to take a smart guess at what the word means.

Let's see what we know about Reid and cupcakes. Well, we know that it was surprising that Reid didn't eat the cupcakes that his mom gave him for a snack. We also know that Reid could eat a lot of cupcakes if he had the chance and that cupcakes were his favorite food. Thinking about what we know about Reid, answer the following.

FANATIC means:

a. Someone who is sad and upset
b. Someone who can't stand something
c. Someone who likes something very, very much

From what we know about Reid, Choice C is the correct answer. Reid is wild about cupcakes! You could call him a "fanatic."

No one can know everything that is on a test. When you are asked reading questions on a test, sometimes you will need to use context clues. Context clues are also very useful in your daily studies! The good news is that there are four types of context clues, so there is lots of help right in front of your eyes. These clues can help you find out the meanings of words.

- **DEFINITION CONTEXT CLUES**—Sometimes the definition of a word is right there in the sentence. The author puts that clue there because the author knows that the word might be new to the reader. Not only do some authors put the definition in the sentence, but they even give you more clues to make sure you don't miss it! They will put a dash in the sentence to make the definition stand out, or they might even put the definition in parentheses. "Bradley wrote out a budget—a list that showed how much money he had and how much he needed to spend—before he decided if he could afford a new bike." Here, the author tells you the definition of the word "budget" by marking it with dashes in the sentence. Or a sentence could read "A geyser is a release of water, gases, and heat from below the surface of the earth." Here, the definition is part of the sentence.

- **EXAMPLE CONTEXT CLUES**—Sometimes you can find the definition of a word by looking for examples of that word in a sentence. The author will give examples that show you what that word means. "Grizzly bears, white whales, elephants, and dinosaurs are all humongous creatures." From that sentence, you can make a smart guess that "humongous" means very large.

- **COMPARE AND CONTRAST CONTEXT CLUES**—Sometimes the author will show you how a word is like something else or how a word is not like something else. Those clues can also help you figure out the meaning of a new word. "Although one of the cats at the animal shelter was healthy and looked like she had been given plenty to eat, the other cat looked malnourished." By carefully reading the sentence, we can figure out that one cat was not fed properly and was not healthy. That is a pretty good definition of "malnourished." Look at this: "When Neil and Glenn decided to stop arguing with each other, Rodney and Riley decided to call a truce, too." Here we see that the word "truce" means when two sides decide not to fight anymore.

- **INFERENCE CONTEXT CLUES**—To make an inference means to use what you know to make a smart guess about the definition of the word. You think carefully about what you have read and also about what you have learned in school and in your life. You use this information as clues to help you. "When Paula found out that her best friend had stolen her homework and had turned it in as her own, she was livid." If this had happened to you, you probably would have been very angry, maybe more angry than you have ever been in your life. This is what is meant by "livid."

Try to use context clues to figure out the meanings in these sentences.

1. William wanted to be a pilot when he grew up, so he read everything he could about being an aviator. AVIATOR means:

   a. A good reader

   b. A pilot

   c. A helpful and responsible person

2. Unlike her sister Martha who spends all the money she has and never buys anything on sale, Clarissa is a thrifty shopper. THRIFTY means:

   a. Being careless with your money

   b. Dressing in boring clothes

   c. Spending your money carefully

3. Mr. Duffy added on a bigger kitchen and another bedroom in order to enlarge his house. ENLARGE means:

   a. To make something safer

   b. To build something

   c. To make something bigger or larger

4. Chuck ate most of his food when the group stopped for lunch and ate the remainder for his snack later in the day. REMAINDER means:

   a. What is left over

   b. Something that is old and stale

   c. A type of snack

5. Living near his aunts, uncles, cousins, and grandparents made Luther pleased that he could be close to his kin. KIN means:

   a. Neighbors

   b. Family members

   c. Friends

6. Billy made fun of people who were different than him, but Kris did not like to be prejudiced. PREJUDICED means:

   a. Stupid

   b. Not being nice to people who aren't like you

   c. Wanting to be friends with kids who speak a different language

7. Just like her sullen brother, Tracy made an ugly face and hung her head down when she didn't get her way. SULLEN means:

   a. Having a bad attitude if you don't get what you want

   b. Being dangerous

   c. Being a twin

8. A huge boulder—a large rock that has fallen off the side of a mountain—blocked the dirt road. BOULDER means:

   a. A hole in the road

   b. A large rock

   c. An explosive

9. Melissa tried out to be in the talent show, but Jolene refused to audition. AUDITION means:

   a. To try to be chosen to be in a show

   b. To cooperate

   c. To try your hardest

10. First one scientist looked carefully at the fossil and then the other scientist inspected it carefully. INSPECT means:

    a. To weigh something

    b. To examine something

    c. To hold something

Activity 45

A Title Is a Secret Tool for Doing Your Best on Tests and in School!

Ivan thought that his day couldn't get much worse until he was captured by aliens! He was walking home near the park. Suddenly, a spacecraft that looked like an airplane made out of red and green Jell-o landed beside him. Two very green little creatures pulled him inside, and the rest is history! "Well," thought Ivan, "here I go! First my bike chain broke and I had to walk to school. Then it started raining and I forgot my jacket. And to top it off, I had a boring language arts lesson. Now, here I am, captured by aliens! What will happen next?"

A lot happened next! The aliens, who thankfully spoke English (and a little Spanish), politely told Ivan that they weren't going to hurt him. They just wanted to learn all they could about kids. "We will keep you for a year or two, but don't worry. You will still keep up with your friends in school because we will send knowledge x-rays into your brain. You will be pretty smart by the time you return."

Ivan didn't really like that idea. Although the aliens were nice, he really wanted to be home. He even wanted to be back in school. He couldn't believe he was thinking that after that boring language arts lesson!

Suddenly, Ivan remembered that lesson. It was all about titles and how they could help you understand what was important. Since the most important thing was to get out of this slimy spacecraft, Ivan began to look for anything that might be a title! Ivan saw a sign on a panel of lights. The lights were all blinking and confusing, but the sign said "Door Control." The sign was kind of like a title. Ivan figured out that the lights had something to do with opening and closing doors. "What do I have to lose?" thought Ivan. So he began to touch all the lights and buttons. All at once, the door on his room opened! So he walked out into the middle of the spacecraft.

Then he saw a sign that read "Library." Again, Ivan paid attention to what was important. "Well," thought Ivan, "this might be helpful." So he went in and, sure enough, there were hundreds of books about the aliens. Looking around some more, he saw a book that was labeled "How to Get Along with Aliens." He opened the book and looked at the title of each chapter. He didn't have time to look at every page, but those titles sure were helpful! Soon he found a chapter titled "How to Escape From a Green and Red Slippery Spacecraft." Reading the chapter, Ivan learned how to get back home. "If you politely ask an alien to let you go home, he will grant your wish!" Now having all that knowledge, Ivan went up to the greenest little guy and said, "I enjoyed meeting you, but could I please go home?" And before he knew it, he was back near the park, on his way home. Ivan learned that titles are his friends!

Titles are short and usually easy to read. They give students a lot of important information to help them understand what they read. This helps them do their best on schoolwork and tests. Here is how they can help!

- A title will give you the main idea. If the title reads "Whales are the Kings of the Sea," you know that the main idea is about the power of whales. The chapter or story might talk a little about other things, but whales are the main idea.

- A title will let you know if writing is fiction or nonfiction. Fiction writing is about something that comes from the imagination, not what really happened. Nonfiction writing is about facts. A fiction title might be "The Day Ruby Climbed Mount Skyline," but a nonfiction tile could read "The Tallest Mountain in Our State: Mount Skyline." You should read fiction to enjoy the story and think about the people and events. You should read nonfiction to learn facts and increase your knowledge.

- A title will tell you important words and ideas to look for. If a title reads, "School is Harder in Japan" you would want to pay attention to the reasons why school is harder in Japan. You would know that is what the reading is trying to teach you.

Now it is your turn to make helpful titles. Below and on the next page are two paragraphs that do not have titles. Read each paragraph and create a helpful title for each one. In the lines above the paragraph, give the paragraph a title.

Title: _____

_____

Just a few miles off the coast of Ohio, in Lake Erie, there is an island that is special, not because it has something, but because it doesn't have something! What is missing on that island? Cars! That's right, there hasn't ever been a car on that island and there probably never will be. Thousands of visitors come each year on ferries, which are large boats that cross the water. When they reach the island, visitors have a choice of how to get around the island. First, they could walk. Things are pretty close to each other, and you can walk to ice cream parlors, parks, and other sights quickly. Or you can rent little golf carts. These run on batteries, not gasoline, so they don't pollute the island. You could also put on your swimsuit and rent a water ski. You could go from place to place all around the island on a water ski, but you would have to still use your feet or a cart to travel on land once you parked the water ski. But no matter how you travel, you can bet on having fun.

Title: _____

_____

Do you ever wonder how grownups learned to do their jobs? The main answer is that they spent time learning and worked hard! To do some jobs, it takes years and years of school. Going to school for a long time seems hard, but if you love what you are learning, it can be fun! To be a doctor, you have to finish high school, go to college, then go to medical school, and then you have to be a "student doctor" for four to eight years! You might not be done with school until you are more than 30 years old. Teachers also have a lot of education, and they usually never stop learning. They go to college and then keep going, even after they are working. They want to get better and better at what they do! For other jobs you need less school but more learning on the job. Russell's father is a great auto mechanic. He went to a high school where he studied how to fix cars and trucks for six hours a day. Then he went to work, learning more by watching others and trying it himself. Now he has been fixing cars for 20 years and he is a fix-it genius! Some grownups figure out that it is never too late to learn. Hector's mother went to nursing school this year. Now, she and Hector spend homework time together.

Teachers Never Stop Learning

Activity 46

Say It Your Own Way!

In a land far away and long ago, there was a knight named Sir Tellalot. Like his name sounds, his job was to be a messenger for his king. In those days, there was no telephone, email, or post office. If you wanted to send a message, you had to send someone to deliver it. If you were lucky, the person who sent a message would be able to write, and the person who was going to get the message could read. But there weren't many schools in those days. In fact, if you found 100 people, maybe one of them could read or write. This was a problem because not many people could write or read messages.

Most of the time, the king would tell Sir Tellalot what message he wanted to send. "Sir Tellalot," barked the king, "give this message to the kingdom next to ours and be sure not to make a mistake. You can't forget anything that I tell you!" Even though Sir Tellalot was rather smart, no one has a perfect memory. Sometimes, by the time Sir Tellalot rode his white horse to the next kingdom, he forgot some of the king's message. It wasn't that he didn't try, but it was hard to remember it all. Sir Tellalot would repeat the king's message to himself over and over, but he couldn't remember everything. As the horse galloped along, it seemed as if the words flew out of his head.

One day, out of nowhere, Sir Tellalot had an idea that made his job much easier. What happened? He remembered that he had a brain! His brain could do a lot more than just remember exactly what the king told him. In fact, his brain was working all the time. It could be used for more than just remembering boring stuff! "I need to put my brain to use to do this job better," thought Sir Tellalot. "Instead of repeating what I hear over and over, I will put the message in my own words. When I do that, the message is <u>my</u> message. If something is mine, I won't forget it."

And that is what Sir Tellalot did. When the king gave him a message, he put it in his own words. He figured out that it was easier to remember his own words. When he did that, he never forgot what was important.

You can do just what Sir Tellalot did when you read or hear something. When you put what you read or hear in your own words, you will make it part of yourself! Think about it this way: you don't forget about your feet or nose (they are a part of you!), so you probably won't forget what you put in your own words.

Samantha had the same idea as Sir Tellalot! She listened carefully to her history lesson. The teacher said, "Our state was founded in 1847. People wanted to come to live here because there was silver, copper, and marble that could be mined from the mountains. By 1850, more than 20,000 people had moved here. Instead of building houses, most people lived in tents. The quicker they set up their tents, the quicker they could search for valuable silver or get a job in the copper mines or marble quarries. Sometimes two or three thousand tents made up small towns! The locals called the tent towns "Sackvilles" because from far away it looked like everyone was living in a sack! To teach the children, all the mothers would get together their books and start a school, even if there weren't any teachers. The mothers would figure out who knew the most about each subject and that mother would tell what she knew to the children. Most kids left school at about 12 years old and helped their families."

Samantha knew there would be a test on what she heard. And even if there wasn't a test, she wanted to learn about history anyway. So Samantha put what the teacher said into her own words!

The year 1847 was a long time ago. In fact, it was 100 years before my grandma and grandpa were married. I saw on their wedding picture that they were married in 1947. People lived here because they could make money and could help their families. They hunted for silver, or they learned to mine for copper. They also looked for marble. (I won't forget that because I will imagine beautiful, shiny marbles being made or big marble statues that I saw in a museum.) There weren't schools like we have today because there weren't any teachers. The moms would get together with all the school supplies that they could find and teach the kids. If one mom was really good at something, then the other moms would pick her to teach that subject. Kids had to stop going to school when they were very young so that they could help their families. I would always help my family, but I wouldn't want to not go to school. Even though I sometimes complain about school, I would miss it! And people had to live in towns made of tents, not houses! They looked like bags or sacks.

Samantha didn't just repeat what the teacher said. She put it in her own words and then the knowledge was hers! Samantha was very proud of herself.

You can also say it your own way. And if the teacher asks you to write about what you just read, you can write it in your own way. So get your brain going and give this a try! Read this paragraph and then write what you learned in your own words!

Today, computers are in many schools. They are used to find information, to type papers, to learn math and reading skills, to make banners and posters, and to play games and have fun. Teachers use computers to make study sheets, record grades, and email parents. Principals use computers to keep track of everything that goes on in school. People use computers because computers are fast and small (they can fit on a desk or even on your lap). But that wasn't the way it always was! Not too long ago (about the time that your parents were your age), computers were very big and slow. They also didn't play games, show pictures or colors, or even have sound. Just one computer would be the size of your classroom and would cost about as much as your whole school! What made computers better? A wonderful invention called the microchip. A microchip could store pages and pages (even books) of instructions that tell a computer what to do. Smaller computers could be made because microchips are about the size of a penny. It might be fun to eat a potato chip or to eat chocolate chip ice cream, but the best chip in the world is the microchip!

In the space below, write what you learned in your own words.

_____

_____

_____

_____

_____

_____

_____

_____

_____

Reading Questions Can Give You Answers

Robert and Ben had been friends since preschool. They had lots of fun together. They also had lots of adventures. Robert was always coming up with wild ideas! Unfortunately, some of these ideas were better than others. And, after a while, Ben had to decide if it was wise to do everything that came into Robert's brain! In preschool, Robert thought that it might be fun to see if the classroom hamster would slide down the playground slide. Robert and Ben tried this out. Their big surprise was that their teacher told them that after their stunt they had to miss playing on the slide for two days. Then a couple of years ago, Robert wanted Ben to help him scare the little kids at camp. "We will make growling noises in the woods at night!" said Robert. Ben didn't think it was a good idea, so Robert did it alone. Guess who got in trouble?

But Robert also had great ideas that worked out fine. Last Halloween, Ben wanted to be a hairy monster, but Robert thought it would be cool to dress like a Navy guy and an Army guy. Ben wasn't sure, but he borrowed his uncle's sailor cap and shirt (Ben's uncle had been in the Navy) and went along. It was a hit! Robert and Ben got more candy than anyone else in the neighborhood. People saluted them as they walked by. One older man who took their picture said, "You look just like I did when I was fighting for our country." Robert's idea was super!

Robert came to Ben with a new discovery. "Oh, no, here comes another wild idea!" thought Ben to himself.

"Ben," said Robert. "I've figured something out that will make us the best test takers ever! When you take a test, if you read the questions first, you will get a better grade!"

Now Ben thought that Robert's brain was going wilder than ever! "That's silly," replied Ben. "You always have to read the material and then answer questions. Why bother reading the questions if you haven't read all the other stuff yet?"

"The answer is easy," said Robert. "The questions tell you what to look for when you read. They tell you what is important." Robert showed Ben three questions from a test. "Let's read these questions and make some guesses about what we need to think about when we read," said Robert. Robert showed Ben some questions.

"Where is the stuff we're supposed to read?" asked Ben.

"I will show you later. Right now, just look at the questions! They will give you clues about how to read the passage."

So Ben took the paper with the questions and studied them. First he read, "What do fish that live in rivers need to stay healthy?" When Ben shook his head Robert helped out, "This question tells you that you need to pay attention to fish that live in rivers and think about their health," said Robert. "If you keep this in your brain while reading, then you can answer the question much better." The next question read, "What is the biggest difference between fish that live in fresh water and fish that live in salt water?" Now Ben was catching on (kind of like catching a fish!).

"I guess I had better pay attention to different kinds of fish," said Ben. The next question asks you to write a few sentences about your opinion of fishing. Ben quickly said, "I'm going to think about my opinion while I read." Robert then gave Ben the reading passage about fish. Ben read through it like a breeze and was ready to answer the questions. He couldn't believe how easy this was. "Thanks," said Ben. "This was a whole lot better than sliding that hamster down the slide!"

Here are some test questions that students have to answer after they read a passage. Look at the questions and then write what clues you might look for while you read. Remember, don't answer the questions, just figure out how they could help you do your best. (The first two questions are completed to help you get some ideas!)

1. What is the snowiest city in Canada? _This question tells me that I should try to find this fact in what I read._

2. How is a piano different from a harpsichord? _Well, I don't know what a harpsichord is, but it must be kind of like a piano. I need figure out how they are the same and different._

3. Explain why Veronica and the queen were special friends.

_____

_____

4. If you could have only one tool that farm families used in 1800, what would you want and why would you want it?

_____

_____

5. What were the two holidays that the townspeople enjoyed?

_____

_____

_____

6. What made Mr. Harper so grouchy?

_____

_____

_____

7. Name three types of rocks found near volcanoes.

_____

_____

_____

8. What would the world be like if the medicine called penicillin was never discovered?

_____

_____

_____

9. What would you do for fun if you lived in London, England?

_____

_____

_____

10. Is it cheaper to make paper from trees or to recycle waste paper?

_____

_____

_____

I can use reading strategies! Here's what I am going to do!

☐ I will remember the difference between facts and opinions.

☐ I will read all of the text.

☐ I will use context clues.

☐ I will pay attention to the title.

☐ I will practice putting what I have read into my own words.

☐ I will read questions carefully.

Chapter 9

Mathematics Strategies

In this chapter, you are going to learn about how to do your best on mathematics tests. When you know mathematics strategies, you will be better prepared to do well on tests.

In This Chapter . . .

Activity 48

Kids Can Learn to Like Those Grids!

"Grid" is a silly sounding word. It is also a new word for most students. A grid is a way to show your math answers on the kind of tests that use answer bubbles.

If you practice how to fill in grids, you will feel better about taking tests. Instead of worrying about how to fill in a grid, you can think about all that you know about math!

Grids have answer boxes and answer bubbles (some schools call these number bubbles, but they are the same). You first write your number answer in the answer box. Next, use that number to fill in the answer bubble or number bubble below the box. Each bubble has a little number in it. Color in the bubble and you are on your way to being a test hero! (Don't forget to color in the whole bubble!) And only color one bubble for each number that you write!

Look at this example. How much is 7 plus 10? The answer is 17. So you write the number 1 in the answer box for the tens place and the number 7 in the answer box for the ones place. Then you color the 1 number bubble under the 1 and the 7 number bubble under the 7.

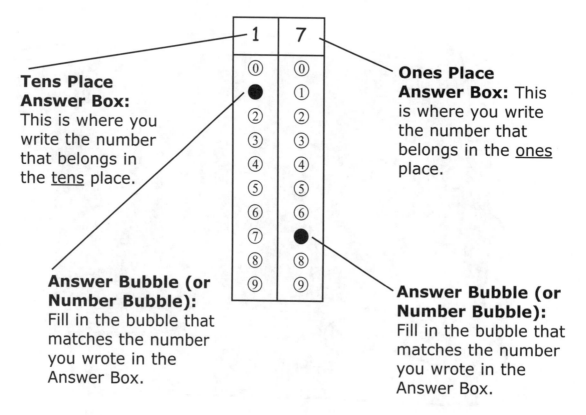

Tens Place Answer Box: This is where you write the number that belongs in the tens place.

Ones Place Answer Box: This is where you write the number that belongs in the ones place.

Answer Bubble (or Number Bubble): Fill in the bubble that matches the number you wrote in the Answer Box.

Answer Bubble (or Number Bubble): Fill in the bubble that matches the number you wrote in the Answer Box.

Now here's some practice! Which of the grids below are correct? In the space provided, solve the math problem. Then look at the grid. Does it show the answer correctly? Circle the grids that are correct.

Thirteen minus ten.

3	
⓪	⓪
①	①
②	②
●	③
④	④
⑤	⑤
⑥	⑥
⑦	⑦
⑧	⑧
⑨	⑨

Twenty plus twenty.

4	0
⓪	●
①	①
②	②
③	③
●	④
⑤	⑤
⑥	⑥
⑦	⑦
⑧	⑧
⑨	⑨

Seven plus nine.

1	6
⓪	⓪
●	①
②	②
③	③
④	④
⑤	⑤
⑥	●
⑦	⑦
⑧	⑧
⑨	⑨

Eight plus three.

8	3
⓪	⓪
①	①
②	②
③	●
④	④
⑤	⑤
⑥	⑥
⑦	⑦
●	⑧
⑨	⑨

Remember to always check your work. Make sure that the answer you wrote in the box matches the bubbles!

Activity 49

Get a Good Start on Reading a Chart

Angel and her grandmother enjoyed doing many things together. They liked baking cookies, taking walks, and doing puzzles. But what they both loved most of all was playing the piano and listening to piano music. One day Angel's grandmother heard that a famous pianist was giving a concert in a downtown theatre and that tickets would be free to kids under 12 and adults over 65 years old. "That's us!" exclaimed Angel, who was so excited she could hardly stand it.

Her grandmother added, "We will go to the concert, but we have to take the bus downtown. The concert starts at two o'clock in the afternoon and should be over at about four o'clock."

Angel had never taken the bus downtown and didn't even know where the bus stopped or it's schedule. She called the bus company and told them that she needed to find out how to take the bus downtown. They mailed her charts that looked like these.

BUS SCHEDULE: INTO DOWNTOWN

BUS #4				
Vine Street	Apple Alley	Connor Blvd.	Fifth Street	Downtown
5:30 a.m.	6:05 a.m.	6:15 a.m.	6:25 a.m.	6:55 a.m.
BUS #7				
Vine Street	Apple Alley	Connor Blvd.	Fifth Street	Downtown
10:05 a.m.	10:40 a.m.	10:50 a.m.	11:00 a.m.	11:30 a.m.
BUS #11				
Vine Street	Apple Alley	Connor Blvd.	Fifth Street	Downtown
5:00 p.m.	5:35 p.m.	5:45 p.m.	5:55 p.m.	6:25 p.m.

BUS SCHEDULE: OUT OF DOWNTOWN

BUS #2

Downtown	Fifth Street	Connor Blvd.	Apple Alley	Vine Street
1:00 p.m.	1:30 p.m.	1:40 p.m.	1:50 p.m.	2:25 p.m.

BUS #5

Downtown	Fifth Street	Connor Blvd.	Apple Alley	Vine Street
5:00 p.m.	5:30 p.m.	5:40 p.m.	5:50 p.m.	6:25 p.m.

BUS #14

Downtown	Fifth Street	Connor Blvd.	Apple Alley	Vine Street
7:10 p.m.	8:20 p.m.	8:30 p.m.	8:40 p.m.	9:15 p.m.

At first, when Angel saw all these numbers and words, she got worried! "I'll never figure out how to get downtown on the bus!" But then she remembered what her teacher taught the class about reading charts!

- **First, look at the chart and ask yourself, "What is it trying to tell me?"** Angel examined one of the charts. She saw that there was a large heading that said "BUS SCHEDULE: INTO DOWNTOWN." Angel felt better because this chart only had information about going downtown, not anywhere else in the town.
- **Use words to help you understand what you are seeing.** Angel said to herself, "I see that there are buses that go into downtown and out of downtown. I also see that there are several buses each day."
- **Ask yourself, "What information do I need from the chart?"** Angel didn't need to know how many buses went downtown. She needed to

know where and when to get the bus so she could see the piano concert. So Angel asked herself, "Where is the closest bus stop to my house?" and "What time should we leave?"

- **Use a pencil to circle important information.** Angel looked at all the bus stops and realized that she lived closest to Apple Alley. When she knew that, she didn't have to think about all the other stops that the bus made before it went downtown. So she circled all the words "Apple Alley" where the chart listed buses into town. Then she got even smarter! She put a line under all the times that the bus left for downtown from Apple Alley. She could clearly see that the best bus was the one that left Apple Alley at 10:40 a.m. This was BUS #7. It arrived downtown earlier than the concert, but that was OK because she and her grandmother could eat lunch at a restaurant before the concert started. Angel also used her pencil to figure out the best time for them to leave downtown. This was on BUS #5, which leaves downtown at 5:00 p.m. She marked the buses she would take with a star.

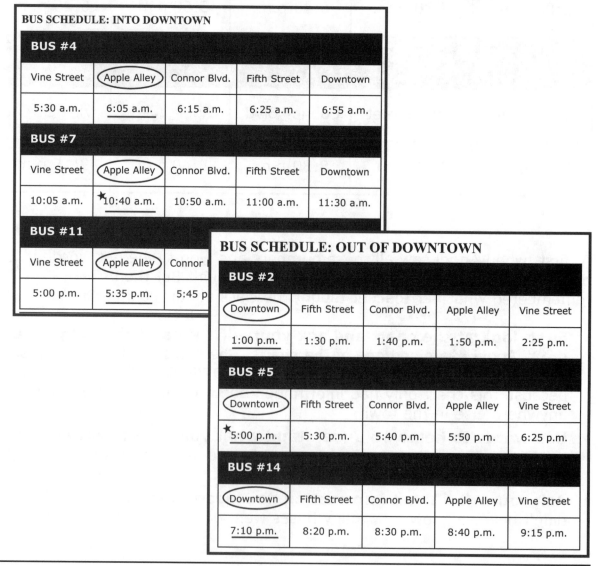

BUS SCHEDULE: INTO DOWNTOWN

BUS #4

Vine Street	Apple Alley	Connor Blvd.	Fifth Street	Downtown
5:30 a.m.	6:05 a.m.	6:15 a.m.	6:25 a.m.	6:55 a.m.

BUS #7

Vine Street	Apple Alley	Connor Blvd.	Fifth Street	Downtown
10:05 a.m.	★10:40 a.m.	10:50 a.m.	11:00 a.m.	11:30 a.m.

BUS #11

Vine Street	Apple Alley	Connor
5:00 p.m.	5:35 p.m.	5:45 p

BUS SCHEDULE: OUT OF DOWNTOWN

BUS #2

Downtown	Fifth Street	Connor Blvd.	Apple Alley	Vine Street
1:00 p.m.	1:30 p.m.	1:40 p.m.	1:50 p.m.	2:25 p.m.

BUS #5

Downtown	Fifth Street	Connor Blvd.	Apple Alley	Vine Street
★5:00 p.m.	5:30 p.m.	5:40 p.m.	5:50 p.m.	6:25 p.m.

BUS #14

Downtown	Fifth Street	Connor Blvd.	Apple Alley	Vine Street
7:10 p.m.	8:20 p.m.	8:30 p.m.	8:40 p.m.	9:15 p.m.

On some tests, you will be asked to read charts and answer questions from information in the charts. The advice that Angel's teacher gave is great advice that should help you do your best. Study this chart and see if you can be a chart detective like Angel.

EXTREME JANUARY TEMPERATURES!

YEAR	HIGH TEMPERATURE	LOW TEMPERATURE
1990	63°	19°
1991	57°	11°
1992	56°	15°
1993	59°	14°
1994	50°	20°
1995	35°	9°
1996	33°	6°
1997	31°	7°
1998	61°	24°
1999	52°	20°
2000	51°	26°

1. What is this chart trying to tell you? _____

2. What kind of information is in this chart? _____

3. Using your pencil to help you, write down the year with the warmest

   January day. _____

4. Again, using your pencil to help you, write down the three years that

   had the coldest January days. _____

5. Does this chart give the temperature for every day in January? Yes No

6. Does this chart tell you about what might happen in the month of February? Yes No

7. Could you use the information in this chart to find the average hot and cold temperatures for "even" and "odd" numbered years?   Yes No

Activity 50

Knowing Symbols Helps Make You a Super Student!

When we read or write, letters and words help share ideas. If you saw the letters "violin," you would know right away that those letters were describing a musical instrument that has strings. It is easier to say, "I am learning to play the violin," then to say, "I am learning to play a curved piece of wood that has strings and you have to run a bow over the strings to make music and you also hold it under your chin when you play." Whew, that would be a mouthful! Thankfully, all you need to do is write "violin" and everyone knows what you are saying. Together, the letters are symbols of what we want to share. A symbol is a shortcut that is used to share information or ideas.

In mathematics there are lots of "shortcuts" that are used all of the time. Most students know that "=" means "equals." No matter where you see it, it always means the same thing. It is a lot easier to write "=" then to write "equals" over and over again.

What's the symbol for equals?

You will see lots of symbols on tests, especially on math tests. If you know what these mean, it will be much easier to show what you know. If you are unsure, it could lead to mistakes, or you could waste a lot of time trying to remember what the symbol means. Both of these problems could get in the way of doing your best on tests.

Taking some time to memorize symbols can help you be a super test taker. You will still have to be a good problem solver, but you will work more quickly and will make fewer mistakes if you know your symbols! Try to see how many symbols you can match on the next page!

Degree	x
Pound	$
Inch	<
Percent	%
Less Than	>
Centimeter	+
Liter	=
Equals	mph
Multiplied By (Times)	" (in.)
Cents	a.m.
Dollar	lb.
Greater Than	tbsp
In the Afternoon	≠
Divided By	p.m.
Minus (Subtract)	÷
Yard	yd.
Does Not Equal	–
Plus (Add)	#
In the Morning	L
Tablespoon	¢
Mile	cm
Kilometer	mi
Miles Per Hour	km
Number	o

Activity 51

Your Grades Won't Be Fine if Your Numbers Are Out of Line!

Numbers can be a lot of fun, but not when they end up in the wrong place! Numbers that are out of place can cause all sorts of problems, not just for kids but for anyone who doesn't carefully line up numbers. Now that can be trouble!

Tiara's stepmother, Mrs. Webster, went to the bank one day to get some money for groceries. She had $700 in the bank, but she only needed $50 to go to the grocery store. "I would like to take $50 out of my account, please," said Tiara's stepmother.

"Certainly," said the woman at the counter. The woman gave Tiara's stepmother the $50 she asked for, but then she made a big mistake. It was her job to fill in a form like the one below. The woman had to fill in the correct amount that Mrs. Webster took out of her account.

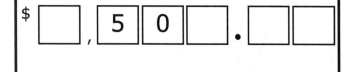

The woman at the bank did not pay careful attention to the place values on the paper. Instead of showing that Mrs. Webster took out $50, the bank thought she took out $500! That was a big problem because now the bank though that Mrs. Webster didn't have much money left. The people at the bank thought she took $500, not $50. It took a lot of time and energy to fix that problem.

It takes practice to carefully line up numbers. Some kids find it helpful to use paper that has small boxes. By putting numbers in the boxes, they can practice lining up numbers so that their calculations come out right. Look at the difference when Quan used special paper to do his math.

The Numbers Don't Line Up!

By Lining Up the Numbers, Quan Enjoys Math Success!

Being neat and careful doesn't make Quan any smarter. He just is able to show what he knows on tests and schoolwork! Quan has a few math tricks for you to try. Work through the tricks below.

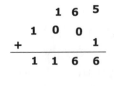

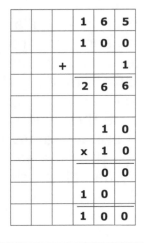

```
    1  6  5
  1  0  0
+        1
  1  1  6  6
```

```
      1  0
  x   1  0
      0  0
   1  0
   1  0
```

Three Is My Favorite Number!

On a piece of paper, write the numbers 1 through 9 three times, lining them up like this:

    123456789
    123456789
    123456789

Then, underneath, write them in reverse order three times like this:

    987654321
    987654321
    987654321

Then add the number 3 in the last row:

    123456789
    123456789
    123456789
    987654321
    987654321
    987654321
+   3
────────────────
    3,333,333,333

Quan's Secret Number Game

Choose a secret number between 10 and 100.	26
Add 95.	+95
	121
Cross off the number in the hundred's place.	~~1~~21
	21
Add the number that you crossed off.	+1
	22
Add the number 4.	+4
Now you will see your secret number!	26

Activity 52

Don't Forget That Math Is More Than Just Numbers!

The year was 1890 and Lauren and Carissa lived in Wild Plains, Kansas. They both had long blond hair and brown eyes and had three dogs. But other than that, they were very different indeed! Lauren and her family lived in a home on the prairie that was very small, made partly out of wood and partly out of mud and grass. When Lauren was a baby, her parents took a wagon train to get to Wild Plains because they wanted to own some land and make a good life for their children. Carissa's family lived in a beautiful house in town. Carissa's father owned the railroad, and the family was rich. While Lauren had to do chores every day after school, Carissa played with her dollhouse and her 10 dolls. She ate cookies and milk, while Lauren only had a biscuit for a snack.

Most of the kids at Wild Plains School were like Lauren. They worked hard to help their families and were happy to go to school at all, even if their school had just two rooms and was way out near a cornfield. But Carissa thought that Wild Plains School was not good enough for her. "We have better books at home, so why should I read this?" complained Carissa, with her nose up in the air. She felt the same way about math. "My father says that you just have to know numbers and more numbers. We go over addition, subtraction, multiplication, and division all the time. Learning all that other stuff isn't going to get you anywhere!" Carissa always knew how much things cost and how much more money she had than the other students and never gave a thought to anything else about math.

Lauren knew better, but she was quiet about her thoughts. She knew that math was much more than numbers and that the more you knew about math, the more you could figure out all sorts of problems! One day Lauren's mother wanted to order some watermelon seeds from a mail order catalog. The catalog said that these seeds would grow best in temperatures less than 30 degrees Celsius. Her mother thought, "That's not right . . . seeds can't grow in freezing weather." Lauren explained to her mother that Celsius is another way to describe temperature and that 30 degrees is really like a summer day. "It's like 86 degrees," she told her mother. She figured that out with a simple formula that she learned in school (Fahrenheit = 9/5 times Celsius + 32). Lauren and her brother had to build boxes to hold grain that they would sell in town. Grain had to be sold by the cubic foot, so Lauren and her brother had to know how to build boxes that held either 10, 20, or 50 cubic feet of grain. It was simple to figure out because Lauren learned that volume is width multiplied by length multiplied by depth. Now she could figure how long and wide the boxes should be. Lauren also knew about averages and that helped her family a lot. They had to buy all their firewood in the summer and had to judge how much they would use all winter. Lauren kept a chart of the amount of firewood that they used each winter month and added it up. Then she divided by the number of months. She proudly told her father that, on average, the family needed 30 bundles of wood each month to cook and keep the family warm. Now her father knew how much to buy when he went to market in the summer. So, while Carissa was busy with numbers, Lauren was solving problems with all of her math skills!

There are many words that help you solve math problems and understand how math can help you in your life every day. Just like it is important to build your writing and speaking vocabulary, it is important to build your math vocabulary. For each of these math vocabulary words, write a brief definition. If you don't know the answer, get some help! That's how everyone learns!

1. Rounding

   _____

2. Metric System

   _____

3. Digit

   _____

4. Probability

   _____

5. Venn Diagram

   _____

6. Grid

   _____

7. Bar Graph

   _____

8. Conversion

9. Circumference

10. Intersect

11. Decimal

12. Percent

13. Denominator

14. Area

15. Mean

16. Pie Chart

17. Place Value

18. Units of measurement

19. Quantity

20. Equation

Activity 53

Make a Math Plan to do the Best That You Can

Michael liked a lot of different things. He liked riding the biggest roller coaster at the fair without holding on! He liked hot dogs with mustard and a little peanut butter. He liked building forts in the snow. He liked hiding in the hall closet and scaring his little brother. He liked helping his elderly neighbor make her garden pretty. He liked reading about world records and weird things about science. But one thing he didn't like, not even a little bit, was math. In fact, you could say that he hated math, except that his parents didn't think that "hate" was a nice thing to say. So he told everyone that he really, really, really, really didn't like math. Everyone understood how he felt!

Michael's parents were concerned about his feelings. They knew that he was smart enough to do well in math, but Michael didn't believe them. "There is nothing that will make me like math ever . . . and I mean EVER!" said Michael. So Michael's parents decided to send him to a Math Camp one summer. Michael would get to stay in a college dormitory, just like a college student. He would study math in the mornings. There were activities planned for the afternoons. He could swim in the college pool, learn to rock climb, or take a cooking class. He could even play on the football field.

Michael wasn't at all happy about the Math Camp idea. "No way!" he told his parents. But he went anyway. And guess what he discovered? He could do math! Michael was amazed. He felt better than if he ate 10 peanut butter hot dogs while riding the biggest coaster while scaring his brother and helping his neighbor! He felt like he had broken a world record. You can also learn what Michael learned at Math Camp. When you do, you will like math and math tests a lot better. Michael learned to be a super math sleuth! (Sleuth is a fancy word for someone who can figure out answers!) He uses seven special steps to solve math problems. Now nothing can get in his way!

---

1. **Carefully read the math problem.** It doesn't matter if it is a word or story problem or a calculation problem, you must look at it carefully. "Sanshi had 12 gel pens and gave 2 to her friend Ani and 2 to her friend Randi. How many gel pens did she have left?" Say it carefully to yourself. Repeat what you read if it doesn't make sense.

2. **Figure out what you are being asked.** Tell yourself, "I need to know how many pens Sanshi had after she gave some to her friends."

3. **Pay attention to information in the problem.** You know that Sanshi started out with 12 pens and then gave away 2 pens and then gave away 2 more.

4. **Use what you know to write a "math sentence."** You would write "12 minus 2 equals 10." Next, "10 minus 2 equals 8." Or you could write "12 – 2 = 10. 10 – 2 = 8." Or you might write "12 – 2 – 2 = 8."

5. **Check your thinking.** Go over the problem again and see if you understand what was asked. Suppose the problem had really read "Sanshi started out with 12 gel pens and gave 2 to her friend Ani and then her friend Randi gave her 2 pens." That would have been a different problem and a different answer.

6. **Check your math.** Go over all your calculations. Did you make a careless mistake? Did you line up your addition, subtraction, multiplication, and division problems so that the columns are correct? Did you make a simple math mistake? If you had quickly wrote that 10 minus 2 equals 7, all your thinking would not have paid off.

7. **Ask yourself, "Does my answer make sense?"** Sometimes an answer just doesn't seem right. If your answer was, let's say "22," that just doesn't make sense. Neither Sanshi, Ani, or Randi ever had that many pens!

Think about this word problem.

> Jevonne, Janita, and Junelle entered a jump rope contest. They were given 1 point for every jump that they made in one minute. Every time they tripped, they lost 2 points. Jevonne made 114 jumps in 1 minute and tripped 3 times. Janita made 102 jumps and didn't trip once. Junelle jumped 120 times and tripped 5 times. Which girl had the most points?

1. Did you read the problem carefully? Circle Yes or No.

   _____

2. What does the problem want to you solve for?

   _____

3. What information does the problem give you?

   _____

4. Write math sentences to help you solve the problem.

   _____

5. Check your thinking. Did you review the problem? Do you understand the problem? Is there anything you don't understand? If so, write it down.

   _____

6. Did you check your math? Did you make corrections? Write down your corrections.

   _____

7. Does your answer make sense? Look at the problem, the information in the problem, and the answer. Does anything seem like it's not quite right? If so, how can you fix it? Write down why your answer makes sense.

   _____

Activity 54

A Secret Code to Math Success!

No one could say when a spy would be needed, but Malcolm was ready. While many kids spent their time on video games and sports, Malcolm explored the world of master spying. Malcolm made sure that he knew all the secret hideouts in his town. Malcolm used some of these to look around with no one noticing. One of his favorite spots was to sneak into an old shed that was near the courthouse. He could get a peek at the sheriff bringing in bad guys and learned what time the judge ate lunch. Malcolm paid attention to anything new or different as well. Once he sort of became a hero. Malcolm was riding his bike when he saw two young and tough-looking guys fooling around with the door of a new car. "This doesn't look right," thought Malcolm. With that in mind, he rode up to the sheriff's office and let them know what he saw. Sure enough, those guys were trying to steal the car. Malcolm had finally saved the day.

Malcolm also loved secret codes. His favorite was simple but fun. He would give each letter of the alphabet a number and then would write what he wanted to say in numbers instead of letters! First, he did it the easy way. He changed the letter "A" into "1," the letter "B" into "2." He went through the whole alphabet that way. "RUN" would be "18-21-14." But then he figured that any smart bad guy could figure that out pretty quickly. So Malcolm found a way to change the code every day! If it were a Monday, then "A" would be "2" and "B" would be "3," which meant that at the end of the alphabet "Z" would end up being "1." On Tuesday, "A" would change into "3," "B" would be "4," and so on. Now Malcolm had seven different secret codes, which he thought would keep those criminals confused for a while!

But most importantly for his schoolwork (even a spy has to go to school!), Malcolm figured out how to change math word problems into math sentences and equations! Lots of kids in Malcolm's class did not like word problems. "How do we know what math to do when we read this stuff?" they moaned to each other. So Malcolm sat down with his friends and calmed them down. "Story problems are just regular math problems, but they are in a special code. Our job is to figure out that code. When we can change the words into numbers, we can get the right answer." This was kind of like his secret code, where he changed letters into numbers!

Malcolm's friend Rusty read a story problem out loud. "Every day, about 1,000 pounds of apples are harvested from Big Apple Farms. But on Saturdays, when a lot of people want to buy apples to make pies, the farm harvests 2,000 pounds of apples. How many pounds of apples are harvested in a week at Big Apple Farms?" Rusty looked like his head was spinning!

"First," said Malcolm, "look at the words carefully. The story wants to know how many pounds of apples are harvested all together. This is an addition problem, so we know that we are adding stuff together."

"OK, go on," replied Rusty.

"So," continued Malcolm, "now we have to find out what to add up! In this problem, we are adding up pounds of apples, but it could be pounds of anything, so don't worry about apples, just think about the math."

"But I love apples!" joked Rusty.

"Keep your cool and let me finish," said Malcolm seriously. "There are seven days in the week," said Malcolm.

"Any little kid knows that!" said Rusty.

"Well since you know that, write down 1,000 pounds seven times, for each day of the week," ordered Malcolm.

"Hey, that's not right!" yelled Rusty. "On Saturday, they harvested 2,000 pounds! So it's 1,000 pounds for Sunday, Monday, Tuesday, Wednesday, Thursday, and Friday, but we have to add 2,000 pounds for Saturday!"

"You've got it!" said Malcolm, smiling. Malcolm and Rusty changed the words into a number equation. It looked like this:

1,000 + 1,000 + 1,000 + 1,000 + 1,000 + 1,000 + 2,000 =
8,000 pounds of apples

"Lastly," said Malcolm, "you could also make this a multiplication and an addition problem." Here's what Malcolm wrote:

1,000 x 6 = 6,000
6,000 + 2,000 = 8,000

To make it easier to add, they wrote the addition problem again, like this:

```
      1,000
      1,000
      1,000
      1,000
      1,000
      1,000
  +   2,000
      8,000
```

Now it's your turn to change word problems into number equations. The first one is done for you!

1. DJ's pet pig "Fudge" weighs 200 pounds. Last year Fudge weighed 150 pounds. How much weight did Fudge gain since last year?

    Answer: The question wants you to find the difference between what Fudge weighed last year and what Fudge weighs this year. Difference problems are subtraction problems. Your equation would be 200 – 150 = 50. Fudge weighs 50 pounds more this year.

2. Rochelle couldn't wait to plant her garden. "I can't wait to taste my homegrown tomatoes!" The instructions on the package of seeds said that it took 90 days from day the seeds were planted until the plant grew ripe tomatoes. About how many months would Rochelle have to wait until she had her favorite tomatoes?

    _____

    _____

3. Jayne and her mother made candles for holiday gifts. Each person was to receive 4 candles in a gift box. Jayne and her mother made 192 candles. How many gift boxes of candles did they make?

    _____

    _____

4. It was 4:30 p.m. and Blake was getting restless. His all time favorite movie was going to be on television at 7:30 p.m. How much longer did Blake have to wait to see his movie?

    _____

    _____

5. Lincoln loves doing pushups. Every morning he does 5 pushups in a row; then he takes a break and does 5 more. When he comes home from school he does the same thing. How many pushups does Lincoln do in a day?

_____

_____

6. Tejas was arguing with Bahru about the weather. "I bet that it will be 10% cooler tomorrow than it is today!" claimed Tejas. The temperature that day was 70º. What does Tejas think the temperature will be the next day?

_____

_____

7. Leandro and Javier were told by their grandmother to cut up 5 pies so that everyone could have dessert at their big family dinner. Unfortunately, both of the boys were too busy having fun and didn't pay careful attention to their pie cutting! They cut one pie into 10 pieces, one pie into 8 pieces, one pie into 6 pieces, one pie into 5 pieces, and the last pie into 4 big pieces! How many pieces of pie did the boys cut altogether?

_____

_____

8. Antwone decided that he wanted to earn money to buy the newest video game. So one weekend he worked as hard as he could, doing chores for everyone. He earned $5 washing his stepmother's car and another $3 for helping her wash the windows on the house. Then he walked over to his his friend's house, and his friend's dad paid him $4 to help rake the leaves. How much money did Antwone earn that weekend?

_____

_____

I can use math strategies! Here's what I am going to do!

☐ I will learn how to fill in math grids.

☐ I will read charts carefully.

☐ I will learn what symbols mean.

☐ I will keep my numbers in line.

☐ I will remember that math is more than numbers.

☐ I will make a math plan.

☐ I will practice working through story problems.

Chapter 10

Answer Key

This section of your book will help you check your answers for the activities in each chapter. Remember, some activities don't have "right" answers or "wrong" answers. The answer key will give you some ideas for a good answer. Compare the answers in the answer key to your answers. Ask yourself, "Does my answer make sense? Is my answer like the answer in the answer key?"

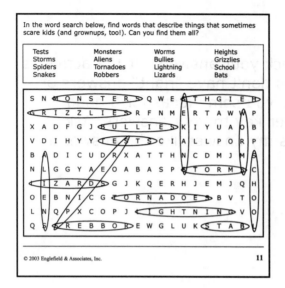

In the word search below, find words that describe things that sometimes scare kids (and grownups, too!). Can you find them all?

Tests	Monsters	Worms	Heights
Storms	Aliens	Bullies	Grizzlies
Spiders	Tornadoes	Lightning	School
Snakes	Robbers	Lizards	Bats

```
S N M O N S T E R Q W E A T H G I E H
G R I Z Z L I E R F N M E R T A W M P
X A D F G J B U L L I E K I Y U A O B
V D I H Y Y E S T C I A L L P O R P
B A D I C U D R X A T T H N C D M J M
N L G G Y A E O A B A S P T O R M C
L I Z A R D S G J K Q E R H J E M J Q H
O E B N I C G T O R N A D O E B V T O
L N Q P X C O P J L I G H T N I N V O
Q S R E B B O R E W G L U K S T A B
```

© 2003 Englefield & Associates, Inc.   11

Getting Rid of Test Stress

What could Ted do to help himself?

_____
_____
_____
_____

What really might happen?

_____
_____
_____
_____

3. April was very, very nervous about taking tests. All she could think about was the chance that she would be so sick to her stomach that she would have to run to the girl's room during the test. If she found one question to be a little hard, she thought, "Well, it is over for me!" April figured that she would be left behind in her grade. "I will never have a very happy life as long as I have to go to school," she thought.

What could April do to help herself?

_____
_____
_____
_____

What really might happen?

_____
_____
_____
_____
_____

© 2003 Englefield & Associates, Inc.   23

Activity 5 (page 11)
Were you able to find all the words in the word find?

Activity 9 (page 23)
Your answers might be different. These are some correct answers.

Ted can think about the things he is good at, and he should not give up on Math. What might really happen is that Ted will study and do OK on the Math test.

April is nervous, so she should talk about her feelings. She should also remember that not understanding one problem doesn't mean the end of the world. What might really happen is that April might get one question wrong, but she could get 19 questions right.

41

Test Success: Getting Rid of Test Stress

Now, check out how much you know about being an active learner. Are these statements true or false? Write a T for true or an F for false on the line given.

1. **F** You should always work by yourself when studying for a test.

2. **F** Watching the clock will make school go by faster.

3. **F** If you ask questions, it means you aren't a very good student.

4. **F** A lot of what we learn in school isn't very helpful.

5. **F** Looking at the floor when the teacher is talking helps us learn best.

6. **F** Don't think about your own ideas because the teacher knows everything.

7. **F** It only takes a day to become an active learner.

8. **F** If you just sit in class, what the teacher says will stay in your brain.

9. **F** There is nothing that you can do about being bored in school.

10. **F** Only the smartest kids can be active learners.

Activity 14 (page 41)

There are different ways that people learn. Hearing learners, such as the football players, understand by listening. A seeing learner, such as the girl watching TV, understands by seeing. Doing learners, such as the kids working in the science lab, understand by doing.

Activity 15 (page 45)

All the statements are false. Stay away from these ideas if you want to be an active learner!

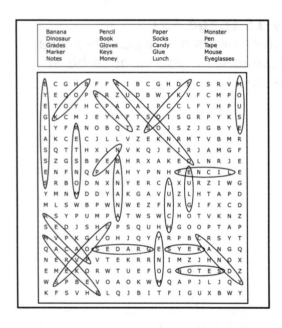

Transportation	Music	Food
Train	CD Player	Banana
Walk	Sing	Milk
Space Shuttle	Concert	Peanut Butter
Skates	Piano	Sandwich
Bus	Radio	Potato
Bicycle	Notes	Ice Cream
Airplane	Dance	Beef
Truck	Drums	Ketchup
Motorcycle	Rock Star	Peas
Boat	Tuba	Cookie
Baby Stroller		Spinach
Tricycle		Apple
Car		

© 2003 Englefield & Associates, Inc.   49

Activity 16 (page 49)
Transportation words are words that are related to how people get from one place to another. Music words are words that are related to music and musical sound. Food words are words that are related to food and things that are eaten.

Activity 20 (page 61)
Were you able to find all the words in the word find?

Chad

Activity 24 (page 72)
Your answers might be different. These are some correct answers. Instead of paying attention to his test, Chad could: listen to the girls talk; listen to the boy's pencil tapping; think about the name on the board; look at the boy's funny hat; look at the animals in the room; look at the dog outside; look at things on the classroom walls; or think about lunch.

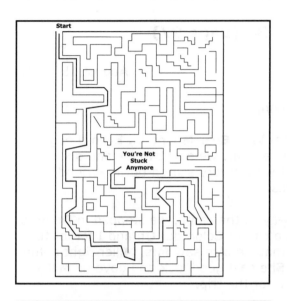

Activity 25 (page 75)
Here's the way to beat the maze!

Activity 30 (page 87)
After filling in the bubbles only, students will find this secret message!

Five families were crossing the country by wagon train. They picked Maggie Reinhard, a girl of 15, to keep a record of their journey. Part of the record looked like this.

	Pounds of Feed Used	Miles Traveled	Type of Land
Day 10	100	20	Rocky
Day 11	110	18	Rocky
Day 12	60	35	Grassy
Day 13	55	40	Grassy
Day 14	105	5	Woods
Day 15	110	8	Woods
Day 16	115	7	Woods
Day 17	50	31	Grassy
Day 18	20	2	Desert
Day 19	25	4	Desert
Day 20	65	29	Grassy

Now answer these questions by asking yourself, "What do I need to know?"

1. On what type of land did the families travel the farthest?

_____

Here, the question asks you about the type of land and the miles traveled. You should only pay attention to that information.

2. How many miles did they travel altogether? _____

Here the question only asks you about miles traveled. Forget all the other information for awhile!

3. How much feed per day do the animals eat on average when they are in

the woods? _____

Here the question asks you about how much the animals ate one day that they were in the woods. It doesn't ask you about rocky days or days in the desert.

4. On which day did they make the most progress? _____

This question asks about the best travel day. The answer doesn't look at the amount of feed or the type of land.

Activity 32 (page 91)
1. Grassy
2. 199
3. $(105 + 110 + 115) \div 3 = 110$
4. Day 13

Activity 34 (page 97)

Test Success: Writing Strategies

- Is there a period, a question mark, or an exclamation mark after each sentence? Is it the right mark for the sentence?
- Do I need to use any commas?
- Is there a capital letter at the beginning of each sentence?
- Did I capitalize important words, like people's names, the names of streets, cities, and states, things that have a title (like Eastwood Elementary School), or months and days?

If you can follow this simple plan, your test scores will soar!

Test Your Skills

This is a postcard from David to Simon. David went to the mountains on a camping trip and wanted Simon to know all about it. Sadly, David was so excited about his adventures that he didn't take the time to check his work. His spelling was fine, but his capitalization and punctuation were terrible! Can you find and fix his mistakes? Circle the mistake and then write in the correction.

august 15 2003

dear simon

hello from wild bear mountain? even though we didn't see a Bear we saw two elk and Six wolves I wasn't very scared but my friend jason was

on our way to the camp we stopped in denver which is a city in colorado oh and I forgot to tell you that we also saw mrs. miller right before we left she said good luck and gave us milky way bars for the trip

next time I hope that you can come with us

your friend

david

There are at least 36 mistakes in this letter. If you can't find them all, ask a teacher or parent for help.

© 2003 Englefield & Associates, Inc.   97

August 15, 2003

Dear **S**imon,

Hello from **W**ild **B**ear **M**ountain. **E**ven though we didn't see a **b**ear, we saw two elk and **s**ix wolves. I wasn't very scared but my friend **J**ason was.

On our way to the camp, we stopped in **D**enver, which is a city in **C**olorado. **O**h and I forgot to tell you that we also saw **M**rs. **M**iller right before we left. **S**he said good luck and gave us **M**ilky **W**ay bars for the trip.

Next time I hope that you can come with us.

Your friend,

David

Activity 35 (page 99)
Find the misspelled words. Put the first letter of each misspelled word in the box to find the secret message.

A Secret Message for Good Spellers

Can you find the misspelled words in the paragraph below? Circle the words that are spelled incorrectly. Then take the first letter from each word that you circled and put it in the spaces below the paragraph. You will make a secret message!

Claudia and Amy are supor friends. They like to plev with their pets, make up games, and they enjoye lissening to music. Sometimes their moms will beg, "Leeve your ears alone and turn that noise down!" Most of the time Claudia and Amy will listen but once in a while they ignor what they are told! Now, they might as well forget goiing to the mall or having a sleep over party! They complained, "We can't be good every houre," evin though they knew what was rite. Claudia and Amy loved being best friends. "I wish we could be sisters!" they would think. "But, even though we can't be sisters, it is great that we will always have each othor."

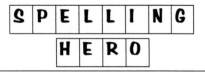

S P E L L I N G

H E R O

© 2003 Englefield & Associates, Inc.   99

Michael made a practice sheet to help him learn to be neater in math. Can you find his mistakes?

```
    1
   43          67          10
+  58        -  4        x 10
  201          27          20
```

Activity 36 (page 101)

1. Michael lined up the 1 in the hundreds column instead of in the ones column.

2. Michael lined up the 4 in the tens column instead of in the ones column.

3. Michael didn't pay attention when he wrote the sign. He should have multiplied, but he added instead.

Test Success: Writing Strategies

(1) The Amish use old-fashioned skills every day of their lives. (2) They build their own barns, make butter in a churn, and sew most of their clothes. (3) My uncle used to make his own fishing rods. (4) The Amish still buy some things in stores that they can't make themselves, but they get to the store in a horse-drawn buggy.

A. MAIN IDEA: _____

(1) A museum is a place where you can learn about many subjects. (2) There are art museums that have paintings and science museums where you can try out different experiments. (3) There is even one museum that has a collection of dolls from all over the world. (4) You have to be careful not to touch or break the dolls. (5) Even if you have to travel a long way to get to a museum, it is worth the trip.

B. MAIN IDEA: _____

(1) Hosting our family reunion was fun. (2) I get sick of my cousins sometimes. (3) My mom and dad had more than 200 relatives come to our farm to meet. (4) Some of my aunts and uncles had not seen each other since they were my age! (5) At the end of the day, we had a picture taken of all of us together. (6) I learned that it is important for families to never forget each other.

C. MAIN IDEA: _____

(1) A lot of people think that taking a plane ride is easy, but that isn't always true. (2) Last summer I went with my stepmom to visit my brother and we went on an airplane. (3) First the plane was late. (4) Then a baby on the plane wouldn't stop crying, and you can't escape from that! (5) Believe it or not, the airline lost my suitcase and I had to wear the same clothes for two days. (6) Going on a airplane could help you decide if you want to be a pilot when you grow up.

D. MAIN IDEA: _____
_____

105

Activity 38 (page 105)
Student answers may vary.

A. (1) is the main idea; (3) does not belong.

B. (1) is the main idea; (4) does not belong.

C. (1) is the main idea; (2) does not belong.

D. (1) is the main idea; (6) does not belong.

You might have great ideas, opinions, and stories to tell (you might even create wonderful movies someday!), but if you forget to use a BEGINNING, a MIDDLE, and an END, no one will understand what you are trying to say. When you are asked to write a story or to share an idea or an opinion on a test, you will show what you know if your writing is organized. Look at the three pictures below. Put these in the right order so that they tell a story with a beginning, a middle, and an end.

2   **3**   **1**

Here are some groups of sentences. In each group, there is a sentence missing. Create a sentence or two that makes a beginning, a middle, or an end so that the paragraph makes sense.

1. It is important to remember to check your book bag before you leave for home. _____

_____. Now I have to do two nights of homework all in one day!

2. Sara wanted to make a special birthday gift for her grandmother. First she went to the craft store to buy supplies. Then she spent hours making a box that was covered in paper flowers and ribbons.

_____

_____. Then her grandmother opened the box and found an even more beautiful gift inside!

Test Success: Writing Strategies

3. _____

_____

"Where is your ticket?" asked the train conductor. "I better rush home and find it!" exclaimed the boy. "Stay on the train for now, son," replied the conductor. "We will worry about it when we get to New York."

4. Tucker lived with his parents on a farm. His dream was to grow the biggest and best pumpkin in the county. All summer long he watered his pumpkin patch. He covered the pumpkins with a blanket in the heat of the day, and he made sure there wasn't a weed within a hundred feet. All of his pumpkins were big and orange, but one was gigantic! It grew and grew until Tucker couldn't move it anymore. It glowed like an orange sunset! On the day of the contest, Tucker and his uncle used a crane to lift the pumpkin onto a truck and drove it into town.

_____

_____

5. Now try to fill in two different parts of this paragraph.

_____

_____. "This water really froze nice and hard on my homemade skating rink," thought Jamie. _____

_____

_____

Activity 39 (pages 107-108)
Here are some correct answers. Yours may be different.

1. When I opened my bag at home, I realized I forget my math book.
2. To finish the project, she put her school picture in a frame and put it inside the box.
3. The boy searched all his pockets but found nothing.
4. When Tucker got to the contest, he was so proud that he had the largest pumpkin.
5. Jamie went outside to look at the skating rink he had put together the day before . . . Jamie couldn't wait to put on skates and hit the ice.

1. _____. On the Fourth of July, people share their pride in our country in many different ways. Some gather in groups in thanks for our country. Many families have picnics and are thankful for their freedom. They enjoy their time together. Most people see fireworks. Flags fly all over the city in celebration!

    a. The Fourth of July is a great time to eat new foods.

    b. Some people like to call the Fourth of July "Independence Day."

    c. The Fourth of July is a celebration for all Americans.

    d. Because the Fourth of July is in the summer, it is the best holiday.

2. _____. Twins sometimes have to learn to do many things on their own because their parents are so busy! They also have to learn to get along and share because a twin is usually nearby. But the good news is that twins are never lonely. Each twin has a playmate all the time. In fact, some twins have their own "secret words" that no one else can share!

    a. It is better not to have brothers or sisters.

    b. Life is different when you are a twin.

    c. Parents who have twins are often tired.

    d. If you are twin, you probably won't be very happy.

3. _____. Some people feel that no animals should ever be kept in zoos. They believe that it is cruel to put animals in cages or pens. Others believe that zoos teach people to understand and care about animals. They believe that this protects animals that live in the wild because people will respect them. Some scientists study zoo animals. They want to use this knowledge to help all animals be healthy and survive.

    a. People have many feelings about keeping animals in zoos.

    b. Zoo animals have a hard life.

    c. It is bad to argue about animals.

    d. Taking care of animals is what everyone wants.

110   © 2003 Englefield & Associates, Inc.

Activity 40 (page 110)
1. c
2. b
3. a

Read the following sentences and write "O" on the line if it is an opinion, and "F" if the sentence is a fact.

1 A) If we paint the classroom blue, it will help everyone feel cheerful. **O**

    B) This blue paint is the same color as the rug. **F**

2 A) The temperature this morning is 85 degrees. **F**

    B) It is too hot to have fun at recess. **O**

3 A) Mustard doesn't taste as good as ketchup. **O**

    B) Ketchup has more sugar in it than mustard has. **F**

4 A) My dog barks every time I put on my Scout uniform. **F**

    B) My dog would like to join our troop. **O**

5 A) Shoveling snow is too much work. **O**

    B) It takes about an hour to clear our driveway of snow. **F**

6 A) My grandfather is the oldest person in our family. **F**

    B) It isn't very easy being old. **O**

7 A) At our school, the kids elect a student of the week, but at my cousin's school, the principal chooses the student of the week. **F**

    B) It is more fair for students to choose who they think deserves to be student of the week. **O**

8 A) My mom does not like to drive my dad's truck. **F**

    B) Girls should buy cars, and they should not buy trucks. **O**

9 A) Our zoo spent $10,000 to buy some peacocks from another country. **F**

    B) It is a better idea to spend money on taking care of animals that are already in our zoo. **O**

10 A) At the beginning of the school year, everyone must buy 10 pencils, five pens, three large erasers, crayons, and at least 500 sheets of notebook paper. **F**

    B) It would be nice if students bought colored markers and tape at the beginning of the school year. **O**

     117

Activity 42 (page 117)
You should mark which statements are facts and which are opinions.

Practice Reading It All

Look at the sentences below. The words are spelled correctly, but the sentences do not make sense. After reading the sentences carefully, write a few words about what was wrong with the sentence.

Example: I can't wait to get out my sled and ice skates when it starts snowing next summer.

Answer: It doesn't snow in the summer.

1. Aunt Karen has a big pond behind his house.

_____

2. The United States has sent astronauts to the moon and the sun.

_____

_____

118 © 2003 Englefield & Associates, Inc.

Reading Strategies

3. If you plan to bake a cherry pie, make sure to turn off the refrigerator after you are done.

_____

4. Our family didn't go on vacation until July although we planned to go the month before in August.

_____

5. My brother C.J., who just had his 8th birthday, will soon be going to college.

_____

6. There are 50 countries represented on the American flag.

_____

7. My dad's car got stuck because he didn't have any water in the tire.

_____

8. Make sure you erase what you typed on the computer so you can print it out later.

_____

9. When my dad and stepmom met with my teacher, I knew I was in trouble because there were four adults against one little kid!

_____

10. I better remember to use my thermometer to measure the distance between my bed and my dresser.

_____

© 2003 Englefield & Associates, Inc. 119

Activity 43 (pages 118-119)

1. Aunt Karen is a "her," not a "him"!

2. Astronauts have not been sent to the sun. It's too hot!

3. A cherry pie is baked in the oven, not in the refrigerator.

4. The month before July is June; August is after July.

5. Most people don't go to college at 8 years old.

6. The stars on the flag stand for 50 states, not countries.

7. Car tires are filled with air, not water.

8. When you erase something, it is gone and cannot be printed. You should save it instead.

9. There are three adults (dad, stepmom, teacher), not four.

10. A tape measure measures distance; a thermometer measures temperature.

Try to use context clues to figure out the meanings in these sentences.

1. William wanted to be a pilot when he grew up, so he read everything he could about being an aviator. AVIATOR means:

   a. A good reader
   b. A pilot
   c. A helpful and responsible person

2. Unlike her sister Martha who spends all the money she has and never buys anything on sale, Clarissa is a thrifty shopper. THRIFTY means:

   a. Being careless with your money
   b. Dressing in boring clothes
   c. Spending your money carefully

3. Mr. Duffy added on a bigger kitchen and another bedroom in order to enlarge his house. ENLARGE means:

   a. To make something safer
   b. To build something
   c. To make something bigger or larger

4. Chuck ate most of his food when the group stopped for lunch and ate the remainder for his snack later in the day. REMAINDER means:

   a. What is left over
   b. Something that is old and stale
   c. A type of snack

5. Living near his aunts, uncles, cousins, and grandparents made Luther pleased that he could be close to his kin. KIN means:

   a. Neighbors
   b. Family members
   c. Friends

6. Billy made fun of people who were different than him, but Kris did not like to be prejudiced. PREJUDICED means:

   a. Stupid
   b. Not being nice to people who aren't like you
   c. Wanting to be friends with kids who speak a different language

7. Just like her sullen brother, Tracy made an ugly face and hung her head down when she didn't get her way. SULLEN means:

   a. Having a bad attitude if you don't get what you want
   b. Being dangerous
   c. Being a twin

8. A huge boulder—a large rock that has fallen off the side of a mountain—blocked the dirt road. BOULDER means:

   a. A hole in the road
   b. A large rock
   c. An explosive

9. Melissa tried out to be in the talent show, but Jolene refused to audition. AUDITION means:

   a. To try to be chosen to be in a show
   b. To cooperate
   c. To try your hardest

10. First one scientist looked carefully at the fossil and then the other scientist inspected it carefully. INSPECT means:

   a. To weigh something
   b. To examine something
   c. To hold something

Activity 44 (pages 122-123)

1. b
2. c
3. c
4. a
5. b
6. b
7. a
8. b
9. a
10. b

Reading Strategies

Now it is your turn to make helpful titles. Below and on the next page are two paragraphs that do not have titles. Read each paragraph and create a helpful title for each one. In the lines above the paragraph, give the paragraph a title.

Title: _____

Just a few miles off the coast of Ohio, in Lake Erie, there is an island that is special, not because it has something, but because it doesn't have something! What is missing on that island? Cars! That's right, there hasn't ever been a car on that island and there probably never will be. Thousands of visitors come each year on ferries, which are large boats that cross the water. When they reach the island, visitors have a choice of how to get around the island. First, they could walk. Things are pretty close to each other, and you can walk to ice cream parlors, parks, and other sights quickly. Or you can rent little golf carts. These run on batteries, not gasoline, so they don't pollute the island. You could also put on your swimsuit and rent a water ski. You could go from place to place all around the island on a water ski, but you would have to still use your feet or a cart to travel on land once you parked the water ski. But no matter how you travel, you can bet on having fun.

Title: _____

Do you ever wonder how grownups learned to do their jobs? The main answer is that they spent time learning and worked hard! To do some jobs, it takes years and years of school. Going to school for a long time seems hard, but if you love what you are learning, it can be fun! To be a doctor, you have to finish high school, go to college, then go to medical school, and then you have to be a "student doctor" for four to eight years! You might not be done with school until you are more than 30 years old. Teachers also have a lot of education, and they usually never stop learning. They go to college and then keep going, even after they are working. They want to get better and better at what they do! For other jobs you need less school but more learning on the job. Russell's father is a great auto mechanic. He went to a high school where he studied how to fix cars and trucks for six hours a day. Then he went to work, learning more by watching others and trying it himself. Now he has been fixing cars for 20 years and he is a fix-it genius! Some grownups figure out that it is never too late to learn. Hector's mother went to nursing school this year. Now, she and Hector spend homework time together.

3. Explain why Veronica and the queen were special friends.

_____
_____
_____

4. If you could have only one tool that farm families used in 1800, what would you want and why would you want it?

_____
_____

132   © 2003 Englefield & Associates, Inc.

_____

5. What were the two holidays that the townspeople enjoyed?

_____
_____

6. What made Mr. Harper so grouchy?

_____
_____

7. Name three types of rocks found near volcanoes.

_____
_____

8. What would the world be like if the medicine called penicillin was never discovered?

_____
_____

9. What would you do for fun if you lived in London, England?

_____
_____

10. Is it cheaper to make paper from trees or to recycle waste paper?

_____
_____

Activity 45 (pages 126-127)
Here are some ideas. Yours might be different.

- An Island Without Cars
- How Grownups Learn to do Their Jobs

Activity 47 (pages 132-133)
Student answers may vary.

3. look for reasons why the two might be friends

4. look for descriptions of tools in the passage

5. look for holidays mentioned in the passage

6. look for reasons why the man might be unhappy

7. look for names of rocks

8. look for effects of penicillin

9. look for things to do in London

10. look for the costs of making paper and recycling paper

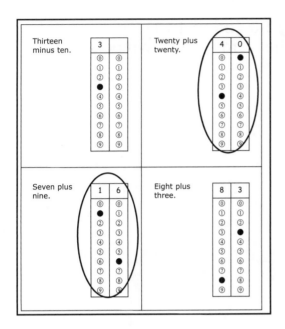

Activity 48 (page 137)
The correct grids are circled.

EXTREME JANUARY TEMPERATURES!

YEAR	HIGH TEMPERATURE	LOW TEMPERATURE
1990	63°	19°
1991	57°	11°
1992	56°	15°
1993	59°	14°
1994	50°	20°
1995	35°	9°
1996	33°	6°
1997	31°	7°
1998	61°	24°
1999	52°	20°
2000	51°	26°

1. What is this chart trying to tell you? _____

2. What kind of information is in this chart? _____

3. Using your pencil to help you, write down the year with the warmest January day. _____

4. Again, using your pencil to help you, write down the three years that had the coldest January days. _____

5. Does this chart give the temperature for every day in January? Yes No

6. Does this chart tell you about what might happen in the month of February? Yes No

7. Could you use the information in this chart to find the average hot and cold temperatures for "even" and "odd" numbered years? Yes No

Activity 49 (page 141)
1. extreme high and low January temperatures for the years 1990 through 2000

2. years and high and low temperatures

3. 1990

4. 1995, 1996, 1997

5. No

6. No

7. Yes

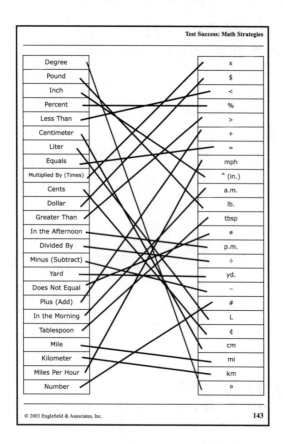

Activity 50 (page 143)
Match the words to the symbols.

There are many words that help you solve math problems and understand how math can help you in your life every day. Just like it is important to build your writing and speaking vocabulary, it is important to build your math vocabulary. For each of these math vocabulary words, write a brief definition. If you don't know the answer, get some help! That's how everyone learns!

1. Rounding

2. Metric System

3. Digit

4. Probability

5. Venn Diagram

6. Grid

7. Bar Graph

147

Test Success: Math Strategies

8. Conversion

9. Circumference

10. Intersect

11. Decimal

12. Percent

13. Denominator

14. Area

15. Mean

16. Pie Chart

17. Place Value

18. Units of measurement

19. Quantity

20. Equation

148

Activity 52 (pages 147-148)

Here are some ways to answer these questions:

1. Remember this when rounding: four and below, go low; five or more, round up.

2. The metric system is a system of weights and measures.

3. A digit is another word for a number.

4. Probability is the chance that something will happen.

5. A Venn Diagram shows what two things have that are the same and different.

6. A grid shows points on a plane.

7. A bar graph shows information on a graph using bars to show values.

8. Conversion is changing from one unit of measurement to another.

9. Circumference is the distance around the outside of a circle.

10. When lines intersect, they meet or cross.

11. A decimal is a number such as 0.25.

12. A percentage is a number such as 25%.

13. The denominator is the number on the bottom of a fraction.

14. Area is the space inside a 2-dimensional figure.

15. Mean is the average of a set of numbers.

16. A pie chart shows data in a circle, with numbers taking up parts of the "pie."

17. Place values include ones, tens, hundreds, thousands, and so on.

18. Units of measurement include inches, feet, liters, gallons, etc.

19. Quantity is another way to say the number of or how many.

20. An equation is a number sentence, such as 4 + 4 = 8.

Math Strategies

Think about this word problem.

Jevonne, Janita, and Junelle entered a jump rope contest. They were given 1 point for every jump that they made in one minute. Every time they tripped, they lost 2 points. Jevonne made 114 jumps in 1 minute and tripped 3 times. Janita made 102 jumps and didn't trip once. Junelle jumped 120 times and tripped 5 times. Which girl had the most points?

1. Did you read the problem carefully? Circle Yes or No.

_____

2. What does the problem want to you solve for?

_____

3. What information does the problem give you?

_____

4. Write math sentences to help you solve the problem.

_____

5. Check your thinking. Did you review the problem? Do you understand the problem? Is there anything you don't understand? If so, write it down.

_____

6. Did you check your math? Did you make corrections? Write down your corrections.

_____

7. Does your answer make sense? Look at the problem, the information in the problem, and the answer. Does anything seem like it's not quite right? If so, how can you fix it? Write down why your answer makes sense.

_____

© 2003 Englefield & Associates, Inc.   151

---

2. Rochelle couldn't wait to plant her garden. "I can't wait to taste my homegrown tomatoes!" The instructions on the package of seeds said that it took 90 days from day the seeds were planted until the plant grew ripe tomatoes. About how many months would Rochelle have to wait until she had her favorite tomatoes?

_____

3. Jayne and her mother made candles for holiday gifts. Each person was to receive 4 candles in a gift box. Jayne and her mother made 192 candles. How many gift boxes of candles did they make?

_____

4. It was 4:30 p.m. and Blake was getting restless. His all time favorite movie was going to be on television at 7:30 p.m. How much longer did Blake have to wait to see his movie?

_____

---

5. Lincoln loves doing pushups. Every morning he does 5 pushups in a row; then he takes a break and does 5 more. When he comes home from school he does the same thing. How many pushups does Lincoln do in a day?

_____

6. Tejas was arguing with Bahru about the weather. "I bet that it will be 10% cooler tomorrow than it is today!" claimed Tejas. The temperature that day was 70°. What does Tejas think the temperature will be the next day?

_____

7. Leandro and Javier were told by their grandmother to cut up 5 pies so that everyone could have dessert at their big family dinner. Unfortunately, both of the boys were too busy having fun and didn't pay careful attention to their pie cutting! They cut one pie into 10 pieces, one pie into 8 pieces, one pie into 6 pieces, one pie into 5 pieces, and the last pie into 4 big pieces! How many pieces of pie did the boys cut altogether?

_____

8. Antwone decided that he wanted to earn money to buy the newest video game. So one weekend he worked as hard as he could, doing chores for everyone. He earned $5 washing his stepmother's car and another $3 for helping her wash the windows on the house. Then he walked over to his his friend's house, and his friend's dad paid him $4 to help rake the leaves. How much money did Antwone earn that weekend?

_____

Activity 53 (page 151)

1. You should answer "Yes" if you read it carefully.

2. which girl had the most points

3. the number of points for each jump; the number of points lost for a trip; the number of jumps for each girl

4. Jevonne: 114 – 6 = 108

   Janita: 102 – 0 = 102

   Junelle: 120 – 10 = 110

   Junelle had the most points.

5. Write down your ideas.

6. Write down your ideas.

7. Write down your ideas.

Activity 54 (pages 154-155)

2. 90 ÷ 30 = 3 months

3. 192 ÷ 4 = 48 gift boxes

4. 7:30 – 4:30 = 3 hours

5. 5 + 5 + 5 + 5 = 20 pushups

6. 10% x 70 = 7

   70 – 7 = 63º

7. 10 + 8 + 6 + 5 + 4 = 33 pieces

8. 5 + 3 + 4 = $12

© 2003 Englefield & Associates, Inc.